28/1

The Career Woman's Cookbook

Also by Bee Nilson

PEARS FAMILY COOKBOOK
PENGUIN COOKERY BOOK
COOKING FOR SPECIAL DIETS
THE BOOK OF MEAT COOKERY

The Career Woman's
Cookbook

BEE NILSON
B.H.Sc. Dip.Ed. S.R.D.
F.R.S.H. M.I.M.A.

Illustrated by Yvonne Skargon

PELHAM BOOKS for
THE COOKERY BOOK CLUB

This edition published 1968 by
THE COOKERY BOOK CLUB
9 Grape Street, London W.C.2
for sale only to its members.

First published in Great Britain by
PELHAM BOOKS LTD, 1966
© *1966 by Bee Nilson*

Printed in Great Britain by
Lowe & Brydone (Printers) Ltd., London

Contents

6 Contents

Introduction

THIS is a basic cookery book written specially for the woman who runs both her home and a job outside the home.

She, therefore, has less time than most to select, buy and prepare food. Meals must be attainable without encroaching too far on such precious free time as she may have.

It is clear that time and energy available for the preparation of complicated dishes can occur only occasionally, even if her tastes run that way. Today, certainly, this does not mean that she is condemned to be a mere tin-opener technician or heating-up addict.

With modern shopping facilities, kitchen equipment and an amazing variety of convenience foods it is quite possible to arrive at a pleasing daily average of pleasant sustenance, and delectable heights of entertainment high spots, with far less time and effort than was possible for women of an earlier generation.

To attain this, forethought and some degree of planning are needed. What is readily available must be known. Some scepticism is useful in assessing advertised qualities or performance of foods and gadgetry. Experience, related to her own needs and tastes, is essential.

All this is not another chore.

Read this book.

WEIGHTS AND MEASURES

ALL MEASURES USED IN THIS BOOK ARE LEVEL MEASURES

Both are given in the recipes because some prefer to weigh when cooking and others like measuring. Either method gives good results provided reasonable care is taken. The measures used in the recipes are British Standards Institute Kitchen measures. They have the following capacities:

1 cup (c) = ½ Imperial pint
          = 284 millilitres (ml)
          = 10 fluid ounces
1 tablespoon (Tbs) = $\frac{1}{32}$ of an Imperial pint
                    = 17·7 ml
1 teaspoon (tsp) = $\frac{1}{96}$ of an Imperial pint
                 = 5·9 ml
3 tsp = 1 Tbs
16 Tbs = 1 cup
16 Tbs = ½ pint

METRIC SYSTEM

In all recipes British weights, and many of the measures, have been converted to the metric system. This has not been done with table-spoons and teaspoons but sizes can be checked against the capacities given in the list above.

The conversion has been adjusted to give practical metric weights and measures which are still sufficiently accurate to give good results. The following figures have been used:

1 oz = 30 grammes (g)
1 lb = ½ kilogramme (kg)
2 lb = 1 kilogramme (kg)
¼ pt = 1 ½ decilitres (dl)
½ pt = ¼ litre (l)
1 pt = ½ litre (l)
⅛ inch = 3 millimetres (mm)
1 inch = 2 ½ centimetres (cm)

TEMPERATURES

	°F	°C
Storage in the freezer	0	−18
Freezing temperature for water	32	0
Simmering	185	85
Boiling	212	100
Tepid or lukewarm	80	30

Oven temperatures	°F	°C
Very Slow	250–300	120–150
Slow	300–350	150–177
Moderate	350–375	177–190
Moderately Hot	375–400	190–205
Hot	400–425	205–218
Very Hot	450–500	232–316

CHAPTER ONE

The Career Woman's Kitchen

THE design and layout of the kitchen, the kind of storage units, the location of food and equipment stores, all these are as important for quick and easy working as any labour-saving gadgets such as electric mixers, automatic cookers and so on. Often much can be done to improve an existing kitchen simply by rearranging the storage of frequently used equipment.

If you are planning a new kitchen or buying more fitments be very critical about points such as depths of cupboards and shelves, quality of drawers and sliding doors, things much neglected in many designs. Deep dark cupboards and shelves are terrible time-wasters.

Some modern kitchens eliminate storage cupboards by having one wall of the kitchen, e.g. the end of a U-shaped kitchen, made entirely of open shelves including a wide work bench with a few shallow drawers, and with storage shelves for heavy equipment below. When not in use, the whole thing can be closed by folding, or shutter doors. The idea is an admirable one for saving time usually taken in opening and shutting doors and drawers. The snag is that if the kitchen ventilation is not good and much frying and steamy cooking is done, the contents of the shelves will very quickly become greasy or damp.

Remember too that labour-saving equipment needs space and it can be more nuisance than help in a small overcrowded kitchen, so do not be tempted to buy for the sake of having the latest gadgets.

GENERAL LAYOUT

The most convenient shape for working in is either the U-shaped kitchen or the 'passage' type with two parallel walls used for the fittings and not less than 4 feet (1¼ m) clear space down the centre.

As far as large items are concerned, the cooker should be fairly near the sink and the refrigerator near the main work bench but not next door to the cooker.

With the 'passage' type of kitchen it is possible to have oven, refrigerator and freezer built in along one wall together with storage cupboards and drawers, with one or two conveniently placed pull-out shelves on which to rest heavy things. The other wall would then be a working surface housing the sink and hob unit and with cupboards or shelves over it.

If space is restricted a conventional cooker is better than a split-level one and refrigerator and freezer with working tops are better than taller models.

With a square or wide kitchen the use of 'island' working fitments is a good way of getting extra working space. Such a fitment can house the hob unit and thus provide access to it from both sides.

Avoid putting a cooker in a corner because this makes using the hob very awkward. If possible, have a stainless steel top to the working surface next to the cooker, for taking hot pots and pans.

HEIGHTS AND DEPTHS OF EQUIPMENT

For the average woman of 5 ft 2–3 in (1¾ m), working surfaces are usually most convenient if 34 in (85 cm) from the floor. This sort of fitment is usually only 18 in (45 cm) deep but it is possible to have an overhanging top to a depth of 3 in (8 cm) at the front or back to provide a deeper and more useful working area. Some cookers are now made for this height of fitment but are usually considerably deeper than 18 in (45 cm) so if you want a flush-fitting cooker the fitments will have to be built out from the wall.

The taller woman will find 36 in (90 cm) from the floor a more convenient height and these fitments are usually 21 in (53 cm) deep but their depth can be further extended in the same ways as the smaller ones.

Wall cupboards above work surfaces should leave a space of at least 13 in (33 cm) between bench top and bottom of the wall cupboard and the cupboard should not be more than 1 ft (30 cm) deep above a 21 in (53 cm) deep working top. Sloping wall cupboards with narrow shelves at the bottom are very useful.

WORKING SURFACES

Plenty of work top space is essential for quick and easy food preparation. Several conveniently placed tops can be more useful than one continuous surface. For example, a working top by the sink bench is important for all sorts of jobs, including holding a small dish-washing machine. Metal topped surfaces by the cooker have already been mentioned. These are the two tops you will probably use most frequently.

A fair sized top to take mixers and other appliances is needed and for general mixing and preparation.

Easy-to-clean formica makes the best surface with metal for the one by the cooker.

STORAGE UNITS

The most common depths for these are 18 in (45 cm) or 21 in (53 cm). This is really too deep for cupboards though not for work tops. Only a few large items of equipment need this much shelf space. It is inconvenient and time-wasting to stack pieces of equipment one behind the other on deep shelves.

Deep cupboards should either have shallow shelves and then something stored on the back of the cupboard door to use the rest of the space, or, better, they should have pull-out shelves like drawers. These can be on rollers for easy handling and have a deep front like a drawer.

Units with plenty of drawers are the most useful fitments provided they are good quality and the drawers slide easily. They are specially useful for all small items and should have more shallow than deep drawers though one or two of the latter are useful for the larger items like cake tins, sieves and strainers. For small equipment allow more drawer than cupboard storage, leaving the latter for large items.

Narrow shelves are also more efficient for food storage but it is now possible to buy sets of drawers to hold sugar and other dry goods. These are usually made of clear plastic so the contents can be easily identified. They can be bought in nests or in single rows, very useful for fitting under wall cupboards. They are much quicker to use and more convenient than any cupboard storage.

For wall storage some open shelves are handy for keeping items which are in daily use. This saves a lot of time. Other things can be hung on the walls at an easy-to-reach height. The things most useful on open shelves or on walls are saucepans, frypans, teapot, coffee maker, tea and coffee containers, salt, spices, condiments, measuring jug, scales, can opener, kitchen scissors, cooking spoons, forks and ladles.

One or two vertical pull-out drawers are useful, especially under the sink to house swabs, soaps and other things used at the sink. This is also a useful way of storing tall objects like oven trays and flat cake tins and racks. Another way of storing tall narrow objects is in a cupboard with vertical divisions like a record filing cabinet.

Awkward corner cupboards or very deep cupboards can be made more convenient by having swing-out shelves or revolving shelves though the latter must be very well made to be efficient.

ARRANGEMENT OF SMALL EQUIPMENT

To save time store equipment nearest to the place where it will be most frequently used.

Near the Cooker Store Saucepans, stirrers, fish slice. Some salt, sugar, pepper, flour, herbs and other flavouring used at the stove. A basin or two. A measure for liquids. Plates and other dishes which will have to be heated for serving food. Tea, coffee and equipment for making these and other beverages.

Near the Sink Store All washing-up materials. Vegetables, colander, vegetable knives, chopping board. Sink tidy, hand towel and/or paper towels, tea towels, equipment for refuse disposal.

Near the Refrigerator Store Jugs to take milk and cream. Glasses for cold drinks. The butter dish. The salad bowl and equipment for mixing dressings. Polythene bags and other equipment for storing food in the refrigerator and freezer.

LIGHTING VENTILATION AND ELECTRIC POINTS

Good shadow-free lighting is essential for easy and safe working. If a central fluorescent light is not enough have small lights over awkward places. Hob and oven lights on modern cookers are a great convenience in many situations.

Ventilation should be good enough to get rid of all surplus steam and all cooking smells. An extractor fan is the best for this but be sure it is big enough for the size of the kitchen, that it is correctly sited, and that it has an automatic shutter.

Have plenty of points at bench-top height for electric gadgets and enough bench space to keep them permanently in position so that time is not wasted in getting them out of cupboards. Store any attachments near-by.

CARRYING FOOD

Buy a good trolley and use it all the time for carrying food to the table, taking dishes to the sink, carrying purchases to their storage place, taking clean dishes and cutlery to their store and so on.

Some good modern trolleys have a hot plate incorporated in the top which is an added convenience, while others are designed specially for keeping food in hot cupboards but the latter are not general purpose trolleys.

CHAPTER TWO

Kitchen Aids

THIS chapter discusses the kitchen aids most likely to be a help in saving time and producing good results with minimum effort. Which aids will be most important depends to a certain extent on the kind of cooking you want to do and I shall try to give some guidance on this point. It is a sound principle not to add anything to your kitchen unless you are convinced it will really do a useful job for YOU. Remember all equipment takes up room and needs to be kept clean so if a gadget is rarely used or is inefficient it is not worth buying.

THE COOKER

For the busy woman the most important points to look for in a cooker are adequate boiling space on the hob, fast boiling with easily regulated heat right down to simmering, and a hob which is easy to clean after spills. The completely automatic boiling plate or burner is the easiest to control at desired temperatures and has the advantage that food cannot boil over if the correct setting for pan and food is selected.

Grills are very popular and a large, evenly heated one is essential. If it is in two independently heated halves this is an added advantage. Some cookers have combined rôtisseries and grills.

You will want a completely automatic oven to enable cooking to be started while you are away from the kitchen. Choose one with a removable oven lining, top, sides and bottom, for easy cleaning. With some cookers the automatic control can also be used for one or more of the hotplates, and for the warming cupboard.

If the cooker is not being completely built into the kitchen fitments it should be on rollers to allow it to come out for easy cleaning.

You will want a heated warming cupboard, and it is an added convenience if this is regulated by the auto-timer.

If you are likely to want to bake pies and cakes while cooking a meal at the same time you will find it a convenience to have a cooker with two smaller rather than one large oven. One of the ovens can be fast and one slow. Sometimes the slow one can also do duty as a warming cupboard.

You will probably find today's electric cooker offers you a wider choice of amenities than other fuels, though competition is fierce and each year sees something new offered by most manufacturers. Electricity at the moment offers a wider choice of automatic controls, easier cleaning of hobs and oven and moveability. The easiest hob to clean is the electric one completely sealed.

Before deciding whether or not to go for a split level cooker study the size of the units in relation to the size and shape of the kitchen and make sure the units are not going to reduce bench working space too much.

THE REFRIGERATOR AND DEEP FREEZE

The refrigerator is an essential item, not only for keeping food at a safe temperature but also to enable buying and preparation to be done in advance.

Some refrigerators have efficient deep freeze compartments and those with three star markings will keep food safely for three months.

Unless you have plenty of kitchen space you will probably have to choose between a fair-sized refrigerator with a small deep freeze compartment or a pair of small table top units, one a refrigerator and one a deep freezer. For an average kitchen the latter is probably better because the units give useful working tops and nearly everybody finds that with experience of a deep freeze they use it for more and more things and a small compartment soon becomes inadequate.

THE DISH WASHING MACHINE

This is a time-saver even when there are only two in the family. Dishes can be put in the machine after each meal, left until the end of the day, and all washed together.

Small machines will stand on a bench or some can be fixed to the wall. Larger models are either fitted under a sink bench or built in as part of a working bench.

ELECTRIC MIXERS

A good strong electric mixer with a variety of attachments can save a great deal of time either by doing a job faster than is possible by hand, or because it can be left to do one job while you get on with something else. Which sort of mixer and which attachments will be most useful depends on the kind of cooking you will do. If you are not likely to want to make cakes and puddings then a cake mixing machine of the larger type is probably not going to be very useful. Instead you might find it better to buy a portable mixer which can come off its stand and be used at the cooker for creaming potatoes, beating sauces, etc. It will also be suitable for doing light cake mixing such as making sponges and meringues.

An electric mincer is a useful machine and it can be bought with attachments for grating and slicing.

Probably the most time-saving of all is the electric blender or liquidiser which will reduce food to purées or liquids in a matter of seconds. Other useful attachments include a knife sharpener, a juice extractor and a potato peeler.

The best outfit is a basic motor unit for which you can buy the particular attachments you will find most useful.

THE PRESSURE COOKER

This is a wonderful time-saver as food cooks in a pressure cooker in about quarter of the time it takes by ordinary boiling.

Pressure cookers are sold in a variety of sizes but a fairly large one is more useful than the smaller sizes. Pressure cookers are usually made to be heated on a boiling plate or burner but some have an electric element incorporated in the base and can be used in any place where there is a suitable plug. This leaves the cooker hob free for ordinary pans. The only snag with this kind of pressure cooker is that the small woman will find it rather heavy to handle.

PANS

Buy only good quality pans with sides and bottom joining in a curve for easy cleaning. Examine handles and lids to make sure all dirt traps have been eliminated and see that the handle is insulated.

Wide shallow pans heat up more quickly and cook more evenly than deep ones but it is a good thing to have a selection of shapes for different needs. Start with one 2 pint (1 l) and one 3 pint (1 ½ l) pan and add to them as the need arises. One or two non-stick pans are a boon for cooking things made with milk, for scrambling and poaching eggs and making sauces. A non-stick frying pan is also a good choice.

Stainless steel pans are the easiest to look after but they do not heat up as quickly as aluminium ones. Copper pans heat fastest of all but require most cleaning.

Pans attractive enough to send to table are a time-saver and the best of these are made either from enamelled steel or glass/ceramic.

KITCHEN CUTLERY

A good set of sharp kitchen knives is one of the best time-saving investments. Keep them sharp for maximum speed and efficiency. These should include a 7–8 in (18–20 cm) cook's knife, a small vegetable knife and a small knife with a serrated edge. Choose stainless steel to eliminate cleaning. If the right kind of sharpener is used the knives will keep a good sharp cutting edge.

Also in stainless steel, have a good strong kitchen fork, spoon, ladle, fish slice, and kitchen scissors.

OTHER SMALL EQUIPMENT

The most satisfactory tin openers are the rotary ones with a toothed cutting wheel.

Colanders, strainers and sieves are best in stainless steel. Round strainers with hooks to fit over the sides of a basin are the most useful.

The best casseroles are those which can be used on top of the cooker as well as in the oven and in addition look good enough to go to table. Choose them without large protruding knobs or handles as these waste oven space.

You will want a measuring jug and set of British Standard Institution measuring spoons. The most time-saving measuring cups are the nests of different sizes from ½ pt (¼ l) downwards. Measuring is quicker than weighing and sufficiently accurate for most purposes. It is however a convenience to have a pair of scales as well as measures, but they must be good ones or they are not worth having.

A food mill is easier to use than an old type hand-grater but an electric one is quickest of all especially if a lot of food is involved.

An electric mincer is very much quicker than any hand one.

BOILING WATER

Most people prefer an electric kettle for this and a good-looking one can also do duty for a hot water jug.

The busy woman will often find it an advantage to have a whistling kettle.

OTHER ELECTRIC EQUIPMENT

A pop-up electric toaster is more convenient than making toast on a grill, whether it is a gas or electric grill.

Other useful appliances are electric hotplates for keeping food warm during service of meals in the dining-room. Sometimes these are incorporated in a trolley. Electric frying pans and saucepans are made to plug in anywhere and so are griddles and waffle makers.

All these gadgets take up quite a lot of room so they are a liability unless they are used frequently and unless there is room to keep them out on a bench ready for use. If they have to be stowed away in a cupboard you will find they get used less and less as time goes on.

CHAPTER THREE

Planned Shopping

ANY well-organized catering, whether for hundreds or **for one, has** to start with a menu plan. From this the shopping lists are made out and the scheme of work planned. This method is essential for the career woman if she is to run her home with ease.

For the majority of people, planning for a week ahead is the most practical, usually starting with the main shopping day. Having mapped out the week's meals, make a list of the foods which will have to be purchased. It should be possible to get the bulk of these in one trip to the shops, storing perishables in the refrigerator or freezer and having very little, if any, shopping to do on other days.

WHERE TO SHOP

Bulk buying of non-perishable foods is best done from a large food store, either using your car for transport or else choosing a store which has a delivery service. If there is no one at home at delivery times, it is necessary either to make arrangements with a neighbour to take the goods in for you or to arrange for the goods to be left at your home at your own risk.

A large store is better than a small one because it will carry a much wider variety of foods than the small shops which can usually only stock the foods in demand in the area. This means their range of convenience foods is likely to be limited and rather unimaginative. You will need a good variety for quickly prepared meals.

The other possibility is to use one or more of the many mail order firms dealing in food. Some of these advertise in the national press. They can certainly provide variety in canned and packet foods and some have an express delivery for certain perishables, but here you have the reception problem again.

If you have a refrigerator and deep freeze, shopping for perishables should not need to be done more than once a week and some manage with even less. The important thing with perishables is to be sure they are of first class quality when purchased and that they are stored properly. The only foods it is unwise to store are cooked meats and other ready-prepared foods which are not either canned, frozen, dried or preserved in some other way. Minced or ready-cut raw meat should not be stored for more than a day either, because in the cutting process it is likely to be contaminated by handling. This sort of meat can always be used for the first meals of the week's menus and the better keepers like chops, steaks and joints left for later in the week.

Fish is another problem-food as 'fresh' fish is seldom good enough to keep for more than a day in the refrigerator and is not fresh enough for deep freezing. Some brands of frozen fish will have to be the main ones used.

For suggestions for using the refrigerator and freezer, see Chapter Four.

BUYING AND STORING TIPS

Bacon Freshly cut bacon has a deep pink or good bright red colour and the fat is white. Do not buy it if it is dark in colour with yellow and blotchy fat. Keep sliced bacon in its wrapping or in a polythene bag or box, or wrapped in foil. It should keep a week to ten days and may keep longer.

Pieces of bacon for boiling are stored in the same way. After cooking, wrap it in foil or keep it in a polythene bag in the refrigerator and use up within about 5–6 days.

Beverages Buy favourite bottled drinks in dozens or cases and store in a cool cupboard. Lager beer and soft drinks served cold can be stored in the refrigerator. Wines and other alcoholic drinks to be served cold should be put in the refrigerator about an hour before required.

Coffee quickly loses flavour after grinding or when sealed tins are open. Buy in tins small enough to use within a week. Unopened vacuum-packed coffee will keep many weeks. If you grind yout own coffee buy enough beans to last a week.

Keep cocoa, tea and proprietary drinks in airtight tins or jars in a cool cupboard. Most of these lose flavour with time so do not buy more than enough to last about a month.

Biscuits Buy several packets at a time and store in airtight containers in a dry cupboard. They can also be bought in sealed tins from ½ lb (250 g) upwards and these should keep longer than packets. The keeping time depends on the condition of the biscuits when purchased but it should be possible to keep a month's supply in good condition.

Bread If you have a deep freezer it is only necessary to buy bread once a month as it keeps perfectly and you can defrost slices or parts of a loaf as required. Rolls also keep very well.

Otherwise buy according to needs and store either in a bread bin or in a polythene bag. Crisp, crusty bread is best eaten very fresh as any method of storage causes softening of the crust.

Fresh breadcrumbs will keep a week or so in the refrigerator or a month in the deep freeze. Dried crumbs should be stored in airtight containers in a dry cupboard when their life will be a month or longer.

Wrapped bread or rolls should be left in the wrapper and there is no advantage in storing bread in an ordinary refrigerator. It may even hasten staling.

Do not let stale crusts and crumbs accumulate in any storage bin as these produce off flavours in fresh bread stored there.

Cakes Store in airtight containers or in suitable wrappings in the deep freeze. Storage time depends on the kind of cake: rich fruit cakes will keep in the freezer from one month to a year, but they should keep for this time in a good tin so freezing is not really necessary. Some cakes can be purchased in sealed tins and these are a good buy to store for emergencies.

It is not wise to try to store different kinds of cakes in the same container as flavours mix, and if crisp things are stored with soft ones they will soon lose their crispness. This applies particularly to items like meringues and crisp cookies and biscuits. But meringues which have been well dried in baking will keep for weeks if stored in an airtight container and make a very useful store for puddings. Large meringue cases can be baked, stored and later filled with fruit and cream.

Canned Foods Most of these have a storage life of a year or more and it is often possible to save money as well as time by buying in dozens of a kind or even cases if there is enough storage room. Any cool, dry cupboard is a suitable storage place. If new stock is bought before the old is finished make sure the old ones are put in front to be used first.

Canned fish in oil or sauce keeps in better condition if the tins are turned over occasionally to keep the liquid well mixed with the fish. Meat and fish will remain in good condition up to five years, provided they are properly stored and the tins not damaged. Canned hams are an exception and their life is short. For safety keep in a refrigerator. Fish in tomato is best used up within a year.

Vegetables will keep for two years without losing flavour and appearance. Milk and fruit are best used within twelve months. After this milk is inclined to change colour and acid fruit may react with the tin to produce hydrogen gas. This is harmless but makes the contents smell.

Cereals Rice and semolina will keep several months if stored in covered containers. Oats have a shorter life and can develop an 'off' flavour if stored too long, but about a month should be all right. With breakfast cereals it is better to buy several small packets for storage unless you have a good airtight container and a very dry store to keep them in. A cupboard above the refrigerator is a good place as the slight warmth helps to keep them fresh and crisp. They can always be freshened up in a warm oven but never taste quite as good as from a freshly opened packet which is in good condition.

Cheese The amount it is wise to buy at a time depends on the kind. All except the soft cheeses such as cottage cheese and those like Camembert will keep for a month in the refrigerator.

Storing cheese—see page 65.

Condiments Salt, pepper and mustard should be kept in covered containers in a dry cupboard away from steam and condensation. Salt and mustard will keep indefinitely but the flavour of ground pepper will get less with time and it is better to buy this in small drums or buy peppercorns and grind your own as required. Ready mixed mustard in jars will keep for a month or longer.

Cream Fresh cream in covered jars or cartons will keep for 3–4 days in the refrigerator. For longer keeping buy jars of sterilised cream or buy tins. Soured cream will keep for 7–10 days.

Eggs Buy at least a week's supply at a time. Store either in a cold larder or in the refrigerator, temperature about 35–40°F. Keep them standing upright with the broad end at the top. This helps to keep the yolk in the centre.

Egg yolks can be stored in a covered dish in the refrigerator, the eggs being covered with a film of cold water. They will keep for a few days this way. They can also be stored in the deep freeze. Whites can be kept for a few days in a covered jar in the refrigerator. In the deep freeze they will keep 6–12 months.

Hard-boiled eggs in the shell will keep for a week in the refrigerator. Egg salads and stuffed eggs should be refrigerated as soon as prepared and not kept for more than 3–4 hours.

Essences Keep tightly corked and in a cool place. Life is almost indefinite though some strength is lost with keeping.

Fats Keep in a cool place, away from foods with strong flavours. Either leave in the original wrappers or wrap in foil or put in polythene bags or boxes.

Buy at least a week's supply but fats should keep for 2–4 weeks, and longer in the deep freeze.

Fish If very fresh it can be kept for 1–2 days in a covered container in the refrigerator, but most fish needs to be used up straight away.

Cooked shell-fish should be used up on the day of purchase. Deep frozen fish will keep for 3–6 months. Cooked fish, other than shell-fish can be stored for 3–4 days in a covered container in the refrigerator or for 3–4 months in the freezer. Prepared fish salads and sandwich fillings should be stored in the refrigerator but not for more than 3–4 hours.

Smoked fish will keep for 1–2 days in a covered container in the refrigerator or for up to a year in the freezer. Fish like herrings, trout and other fat fish do not keep in good condition as long as white fish.

Pickled fish bought loose at the delicatessen can be stored for a day or two in the refrigerator in a covered container.

Flours and Starches Store in the same way as cereals. Self-raising flour must be kept dry to preserve its raising action. Whole wheatmeal flours will not keep as long as white flours.

Fruits: Candied and Glacé Most useful ones are candied or glacé pineapple, cherries, crystallised ginger and candied peel. Buy in as large quantities as you want and store in airtight containers to avoid drying out which makes them hard and tough.

Fruit: Dried The storage life is long, so buy in 2 lb lots or more and store in covered containers in a dry cool cupboard. If it is purchased in cartons or polythene bags store in these and empty into a container when the packet is opened.

Fruit: Fresh This is one of the foods it is wise to choose personally but, except in the soft fruit season, once a week buying should be adequate. If you want fruits like banana and pears to be in top condition by the end of your shopping week, buy the bananas still tipped with green and the pears slightly unripe. Both these will ripen at ordinary room temperature.

Soft fruits will keep for 2–3 days if stored in a covered container in the refrigerator, but they should be firm-ripe when bought or they may develop mould. In a deep freeze they will keep for 6–9 months.

Stone fruits (plums, etc.) will keep 3–6 days in a covered container in the refrigerator or 6–9 months in a deep freeze.

Citrus fruits will keep for at least a week at ordinary room temperature but if you want to store them longer put them in a polythene bag or covered dish in the refrigerator when they will keep for 2 weeks or more. Citrus fruit juice can be stored in the deep freeze for 3–6 months.

Whole pineapple will keep for several days at ordinary room temperature but up to ten days in a covered container in the refrigerator. Cut pineapple will keep in a covered dish in the refrigerator for 3–6 days or 6–9 months in a deep freeze.

Good quality apples and pears should keep in good condition for a week or more at ordinary room temperature but for longer storage either a cool larder is needed or a covered dish in the refrigerator. Peeled and sliced apples and apple pureé will keep for 6–9 months in the deep freeze.

If melon is fully ripe and you do not want to use it straight away, store it in a tightly covered container in the refrigerator. Cut melon can be stored in a covered container for 3–6 days in the refrigerator, or for 3–6 months in the deep freeze.

Game see Poultry.

Herbs Washed fresh herbs will keep for a week or more in a covered container in the refrigerator.

Dried herbs should be stored in airtight containers and should be renewed every year as they gradually lose flavour.

Chopped fresh herbs can be stored in small bags in the freezer.

Jams, Jellies and Marmalade Store in a cool, dry cupboard. Unless it is to be used up quickly tinned jam is best turned out into a covered jar.

Prepared pudding jellies should be stored in the refrigerator as should meat and aspic jellies and just brought out in time to come to room temperature before serving.

Ices and Ice-cream Store in the ice cube compartment of the refrigerator for up to 1 day or up to 3 months in the freezer, in a suitable covered container.

Meat The length of time meat will keep depends on its quality and freshness when purchased.

Plan the week's menus so that meats which are poor keepers will be used at the beginning, relying on the better keepers and the deep freeze or preserved or canned meat for the end of the week.

Sliced cold cooked meat, if purchased ready cooked, should be used within 24 hours. Home-cooked meat should be cooled as quickly as possible and then put into a polythene bag or box or other suitable container and stored in the refrigerator where it will keep for 2–6 days. Sliced, cold meats from a home-cooked piece can be deep frozen for a week or two but have a tendency to dry out. Cooked sausages, like liver sausage and salami, when purchased whole will keep for a good week in the refrigerator.

Raw minced meat should be used up within 24 hours. Keep it in the refrigerator, spread out in a dish with a piece of foil on top, but not sealed. In the freezer it will keep 3–4 months.

Meat sold cut in small pieces for stewing and pies should be treated in the same way as minced meat.

Raw roasts, steaks, chops and other cuts will keep from 2–5 days depending on the condition when purchased. In general, lamb and beef are the best keepers; pork and veal more difficult. Store in the refrigerator in a suitable container but do not seal as this tends to develop off flavours. In the freezer, beef and lamb will keep for 6–9 months; pork and veal 3–6 months and smoked ham 1–2 months.

Raw offal should be stored in the refrigerator in the same way as raw meat but it will not keep for more than 1–2 days. In the deep freeze it will keep 3–4 months.

Ready-made meat pies should be used within 24 hours. Home-made ones should be cooled quickly and then stored in the refrigerator in covered containers when they will keep for 2–3 days. For storage in the freezer the meat is usually cooked first, cooled rapidly and then covered with pastry which is not cooked before freezing. These will keep 2–3 months.

Stews and casseroles should be cooled and stored in covered containers in the refrigerator for not more than 2–3 days. In the freezer they will keep for 2–3 months. In either case be sure they are boiled for a few minutes before serving.

Meat sold ready frozen can be kept for 1–2 days in the refrigerator but should be used as soon as thawed. In a freezer it will keep for 3–4 months.

Canned meat should be stored in a cool dry cupboard. The only ones needing refrigerated storage are small tins of ham. When meat is to be served cold refrigeration in the can for a few hours will make it firmer for easy slicing. It is a good idea to keep one such tin in the refrigerator for an emergency.

Milk Store milk in the refrigerator in the original containers and keep them closed. It will keep for 3–4 days, or longer if it is sterilised milk. Cultured milks like yoghurt will keep 7–10 days, butter milk the same.

Canned milks should be stored in a cool dry cupboard, refrigerating any required for whipping as a cream substitute.

Nuts Nuts purchased in the shell have the longest life. Store in a cool dry place. Shelled nuts will keep several months if stored in covered containers. Blanched nuts should be quite dry before storing in covered containers and they will keep for several weeks. Ground nuts quickly lose flavour even when stored in airtight containers, so use up within a few weeks or store blanched nuts and grind as required in a mechanical grinder.

Oil Keeps well in a cool, dark cupboard so buy enough to last at least a month.

Pasta Except for things like ravioli these keep for several weeks either in the original packets or in a covered container. Ravioli should be used on the day of purchase. Store canned pasta as other canned foods.

Pastry and Pies Raw pastry ready for rolling can be stored for a day or two in the refrigerator or for several months in the deep freeze. Fruit pies and flan cases can be stored in the freezer in the raw state.

Ready mixes for pastry should be stored in a cool cupboard in the original package. Home-made ready mix can be stored in a covered jar or polythene bag in a cool cupboard or in the refrigerator.

Unfilled cooked flan cases can be stored in covered boxes or tins. Store cooked fruit pies and tarts in a cool cupboard or in the refrigerator. Pies with meat, fish or egg fillings should be stored in the refrigerator.

Pickles, Chutneys, etc. These keep for 1–2 years so buy large jars and store in a cool, dry cupboard.

Poultry Fresh poultry should be cleaned, rinsed and dried. Then wrap loosely in polythene or foil and store in the refrigerator where it should keep for 2–3 days. In a freezer poultry will keep for 6–9 months. Pieces of poultry can be stored in the same way.

Pre-prepared stuffing should be put in the refrigerator as soon as mixed and then stuff the bird just before cooking it.

Cooked poultry should have the stuffing removed, cooled as quickly as possible: wrap stuffing and bird separately before storing in the refrigerator. It should keep 2–3 days in the refrigerator or 6 months in the freezer. Poultry pies and other cooked dishes should be cooled quickly and then covered and stored in the refrigerator for not longer than a day. They will keep 6 months in the freezer.

Puddings Milk puddings, custards, jellies and other puddings made with milk and eggs should be stored in the refrigerator. Most of those with a sponge base are suitable for the freezer.

Raising Agents Baking powder, bicarbonate of soda and cream of tartar all keep several months if stored in airtight containers in a dry cupboard.

Ready Mixes Cake, pastry and pudding mixes bought in packets should be stored in these in a cool dry cupboard. Home-made mixes can be stored in covered containers or in polythene bags and will keep in a cool cupboard for several weeks, longer in the refrigerator.

Sauces Ready-made bottled sauces keep for many months so either buy large bottles or several small ones at a time. Store in a cool, dry cupboard.

Most home-made sauces can be stored satisfactorily so it is a time-saver to make more than enough for one meal and store the rest. For short periods, after cooling quickly, store the sauce in a covered container in the refrigerator. For longer storage, use the deep freeze. Mayonnaise should not be put in the refrigerator and it is a waste of space to store French dressing there.

White and brown roux can be made in bulk and stored in portions ready for making quick sauces—see page 54.

Soups Packet and canned soups should be stored in a cool, dry cupboard. Home-made soups may be cooled quickly and stored in the refrigerator in covered containers for 2–3 days. Be sure to boil them for several minutes before serving. Most soups can also be deep frozen as can stock. It saves freezer space if these are made fairly concentrated. They can have water added during heating.

Spices These should be stored in tightly covered containers to stop loss of flavour and will then keep for many weeks.

Sugars, Honey and Syrups All these sweet things have a long storage life and several months' supply can be bought at a time. Store in a cool dry cupboard. After packets of sugar have been opened it is advisable to put them in a covered container. Opened jars of honey should have the lid replaced after use or use a piece of foil for a lid.

Vegetables If you have a dark, cool shed or cellar, potatoes and root vegetables can be purchased in bulk and kept for several weeks or even longer. Otherwise buy a week's supply at a time. Root vegetables like carrots, turnips, parsnips, etc., can be cleaned and put in a covered dish or in polythene bags in the refrigerator when they will keep for two weeks or more.

Green vegetables can be prepared, drained and stored in the same way for at least a week. Salad vegetables will keep in the same way and it is time-saving to prepare them all at once and then have the ingredients ready to make a salad in moments.

Firm tomatoes will keep several days in a cool cupboard. For longer storage keep them in a covered container in the refrigerator where they will keep a week or longer, according to quality.

Vegetables will keep for 6–9 months in the freezer and a good supply of these plus fresh salad vegetables in the refrigerator will take care of most requirements.

Onions and garlic keep well in any dry place so buy for several weeks at a time.

Cooked vegetables can be kept in covered containers in the refrigerator.

Dried and dehydrated vegetables will keep indefinitely either in the original packets or in covered containers in a dry cupboard.

CHAPTER FOUR

Making the Refrigerator and Freezer work for you

THERE are two important ways in which the refrigerator and freezer can be used to help the busy cook. First is to use them as stores for food for a week or more so that shopping time can be reduced to the minimum. The second way is to use them to store food you have prepared in advance for later meals. For example, when the weekly menu plan has been made it is a good idea to set aside part of one evening or part of the week-end to prepare foods for future use. There are so many which will keep perfectly for several days or longer. Also, when cooking food for a current meal, it is often possible to make double the recipe without much more effort and the extra can be stored in the refrigerator or in the deep freeze for later use.

In this chapter are suggestions for getting the best out of the refrigerator and freezer by both these means.

TIPS ON USING THE REFRIGERATOR

1. Keep the maker's instruction book on the cookery book shelf and follow the recommendations for operation, cleaning and general care.

2. Do not attempt to store anything but food which is fresh and in good condition. A refrigerator will not make poor food good, but will preserve the quality of good food.

3. Never put warm food in the refrigerator in the mistaken belief that it will cool more quickly. Warm food will raise the temperature of the other food in the compartment and will cause steaming and dampness. It is much better to allow the food to cool to room temperature first. This process may be hastened by standing the container in cold water, with some ice cubes or by putting the food in a cold, airy place.

4. It is very important to cover all food and, with the exception of fresh meat, the cover should be a good tight one. This prevents evaporation of moisture which happens in the refrigerator in the same way as it does if food is left uncovered in the kitchen or larder. The moisture is deposited on the freezing unit to make frost which hinders the efficient operation of the refrigerator. The air in a refrigerator is circulating all the time and carries flavours from one uncovered food to another and this can be disastrous, giving most peculiar flavours to otherwise bland foods.

WAYS OF COVERING FOOD

Any kind of container with a fitting lid can be used and it is often convenient to store food in a container in which it will subsequently be cooked, e.g. a casserole. Containers without lids can have a foil one made simply by pressing a piece of foil over the top and against the sides. This is the quickest and easiest cover and can be left on for cooking.

Foil is also invaluable for wrapping food and, if you can spare the time to wash it, can be used a second time but usually not more than this as it soon develops lots of minute holes.

Polythene bags too are useful but these need to be washed and dried for re-use and it is more time-consuming than washing foil.

Plastic boxes with lids are more costly to buy but easier to wash.

The most time-saving choice is the covered box or other container supplemented with foil wrapping for the small and awkwardly shaped foods.

Canned foods which have been opened may be left in the cans but cover with a foil lid.

Ready prepared and washed vegetables purchased in polythene

B

packs can be put in the refrigerator as they are and so can cheese, bacon and other foods packed in a similar way. Cottage cheese and other foods in cartons can be stored in the carton but keep the lid on.

Suggestions for storing individual foods will be found in the previous chapter: PLANNED SHOPPING.

Some suggestions for foods which can be prepared in advance and stored in the refrigerator for later use

Sauces of all kinds; see page 53–61

White and brown roux for thickening sauces; see page 54

Hard-boiled eggs

Whipped cream

Cooked meat and poultry to be served cold

Cooked fish to be made into salads or reheated in a sauce

Grated cheese

Salad foods ready washed, drained and stored in covered dishes

Prepared vegetables of all kinds

Prepared fruits of all kinds

Prepared soups and stocks

Pastry ready mixed for rolling; or it may be rolled and shaped and stored thus for immediate baking. Fruit pies and tarts from fresh fruit can be prepared in advance in this way.

A wide variety of cold sweets. They take up less space if stored in a single large container and can then be put in individual ones before serving.

Batters ready mixed for coating foods or making pancakes.

Garnishes for hot dishes such as chopped and whole parsley, parsley butter, watercress and other prepared vegetable garnishes.

Prepared sandwiches and sandwich spreads.

Biscuit mixtures can be made and stored in a roll, then slice and cook.

Yeast doughs can be risen slowly in the refrigerator and baked when convenient.

Most items suitable for an hors d'oeuvre can be pre-prepared and stored.

Grapefruit and other citrus fruits can be prepared in advance as can fruit juices.

Uncooked flan cases store well.

Beverages to be served cold, including iced tea and coffee.

Suggestions for useful foods to store in the freezer The quality of food sold from the deep freeze varies considerably. In general, the least satisfactory are the ready-cooked foods which simply need to be re-heated. It is very rare for these not to taste like twice cooked or re-heated food unless a micro-wave oven is used.

It is more satisfactory to store the raw material suitable for quick cooking, or raw materials which can be removed from the freezer to refrigerator to defrost during the day ready for cooking at night. The busy woman will usually find that small pieces of meat such as chops, steaks and hamburgers are more practical than larger pieces which require long defrosting before cooking. See also page 89.

Chicken pieces are usually more useful than a whole chicken. The varieties of fish which can be cooked while still frozen are useful though it will generally be found that the quality is better if the fish is allowed to defrost first.

A wide variety of frozen vegetables should be kept for these not only save preparation time but also cook very quickly and none of them need to be defrosted.

Fruits to be eaten raw need to be defrosted. Ready-prepared pies and tarts with uncooked pastry can go straight into the oven from the freezer and small ones are very useful for quick meals.

Meat and poultry pies have to be made with a cooked filling and these frequently taste twice-cooked, as do most casseroles and other cooked dishes. Items like curries and goulashes and any casserole or stew which you know stands re-heating well will usually be satisfactory frozen, though not if they contain potatoes. The dish can be cooked in a casserole lined with foil, cooled quickly, then frozen and the foil lifted out with the frozen contents and put in a polythene bag for storage. When it is to be re-heated, the food and foil can be returned to the original casserole. Dishes of this kind should all be brought to the boil before they are served. This can take some time if the quantity of food is large. Use a hotter oven than you would for the original cooking.

Sauces freeze well but require care and attention during re-heating. It is more practical to make and store the roux for thickening hot liquids, or use refrigeration storage for shorter periods.

Bread is one of the most useful things for the busy woman to store as this can be very quickly ready for use and is always fresh. Sliced bread is useful for toast as only a few slices need be removed at a time. The bread can be toasted frozen and will take only a minute or so longer than unfrozen bread. Rolls can be re-heated in a moderate oven for 10–15 mins. Loaves are best defrosted still in their bags. If a loaf is taken out in the morning and left for evening use it will be like new bread. Buns and croissants also freeze well.

Other foods which you can prepare extra quantities of when cooking are apple sauce, fruit purées, fruit juices, chopped parsley and other herbs for use in sauces and savoury dishes, sandwiches, steamed and baked sponge puddings and cakes. Many cold sweets such as whips and mousses can be frozen but require some time to defrost, preferably in the refrigerator. Take them out of the freezer in the morning and put them in the refrigerator for use in the evening. The same thing applies to using raw frozen fruit.

Ices and iced puddings are usually sufficiently thawed if removed from the freezer about 15–20 minutes before required but the time will depend on kitchen temperature. They are amongst the most useful sweet courses to store in the freezer. Ice-cream may be stored in the refrigerator for short periods with the control at normal. If it is to be stored for more than a few hours it is better to store the unfrozen mixture and then freeze before required or, better still, freeze and store in the deep freeze.

TIPS ON USING THE FREEZER

1. Keep the makers' instruction book on the cookery book shelf for easy reference and follow the recommendations for operating, cleaning and general care.

2. The length of time frozen food can be stored depends on the temperature in the freezer. For long storage of a month or more this should be 0°F. or below. For freezing your own products successfully the freezer should go down to −10°F.

3. It is essential to buy frozen food from a dealer who looks after his stock and stores it at the correct temperature. Food which is kept at too high a temperature will quickly deteriorate and if food has been re-frozen after thawing it will be of poor quality and may even be dangerous.

Suggestions for safe storage times are given with the individual foods in the previous chapter: PLANNED SHOPPING.

4. For home-frozen food it is essential to have the correct type of container or wrapper. It must be moisture and vapour-proof. The

most useful are the special freezer quality plastic bags and plastic boxes specially made for freezer use. The latter are more costly than bags but have a longer life and are easier to wash and re-use. When boxes are used the food should fill the box so that when it is frozen there is the minimum air space. Because liquids expand when frozen boxes should be filled ½–1 in (1–3 cm) from the top to allow for this. When food is put into bags as much air as possible should be squeezed out before the bag is sealed.

5. For labelling foods, special grease pencils and special labels are needed: or write on ordinary labels with the grease pencil and fasten the label on with the special transparent tape sold for use in the freezer.

6. Food to be frozen should first be chilled in the refrigerator. Do not attempt to freeze more than 2–3 lb (1–1 ½ kg) of food per cubic foot (30 cu cm) of freezer space per 24 hours.

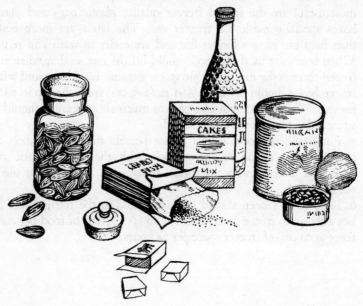

CHAPTER FIVE

Short Cuts

Much traditional cooking takes time because many ingredients have to be prepared before the actual cooking process can begin. One of the best ways of saving time, therefore, is to use short cuts in preparation. By this I mean using ready or partially prepared ingredients or the substitution of ready-prepared ingredients for the raw material.

Every year more and more aids to quicker cooking appear on the market and all those of good quality should be kept in the career woman's store cupboard. By using such aids much more interesting foods can be prepared than by the more obvious use of completely finished canned, frozen or other dishes.

The following list includes those generally available at the time of writing together with some suggestions for using them.

Almonds Available ready blanched and split (flaked) or as nibs.

Breadcrumbs Many different makes of dried crumbs are sold in packets—also some makes of breakfast cereals are sold as crumbs. In addition, for variety of flavour and texture, wheat germ or rolled oats can be used instead. Fresh breadcrumbs can sometimes be purchased but if not are easily made from stale bread if you have a mechanical grinder. Then store them in polythene bags or boxes in weighed and labelled amounts in the deep freeze.

Cakes Use ready mixes and quick mix methods, see pages 210–19; or buy deep frozen or other ready-made cakes of which there is a wide variety, many of good quality.

Cheese, Grated Always keep some grated cheese in stock. Parmesan is sold in small polythene packets or in drums. Other grated cheese is sold by some shops, either in packets or by the ounce. Use it in sauces, to sprinkle on vegetables and savoury dishes and to hand separately to sprinkle on soup at table. It is also useful for adding to sandwich fillings, scrambled eggs and omelets and for pasta dishes.

Fat melted. Use oil instead, unless the flavour of butter is essential to the dish.

Fish Ask the fishmonger to do any necessary boning and filleting, or buy fresh or frozen fillets.

Ice-Cream Use ready-mixes and add your own flavour or use quick recipes; see page 187. Commercial ice-creams are made in a wide variety of flavours but not all shops stock a wide range. Some are available from the deep freeze. Use these as a base for sundaes adding your own sauces, fruit, nuts, etc.

Lemon Juice Canned has the best flavour, or use bottled.

Meat Ask the butcher to cut it up for you if you want small pieces for stews, casseroles and pies, or to mince it for other dishes, but only if you are going to use it up straight away. He will also bone joints or chine them for you.

Always cook roast meat at low temperatures: 325°F, to avoid

splashing the oven and reduce subsequent cleaning. Alternatively, wrap the meat in foil and cook at 425° F., see Meat, page 91.

Onions Use de-hydrated onion for all cooked dishes.

Parsley and other Herbs Use a mechanical chopper for fresh herbs or snip with kitchen scissors. This coarser chopping often produces a better flavour and appearance.

Pastry Buy packet ready-mixes (or make your own mix) or buy ready-to-roll pastry from the deep freeze or use the quick method with oil or melted fat; see page 196.

Pies Use ready-made fillings, e.g. lemon and fruit, or use frozen fruit.

Potatoes, mashed Use potato powders for quick mashed and for thickening soups and casseroles. Use a potato ricer for quickly turning boiled into mashed.

Puddings, Milk Use canned ones and add individual touches; see pages 176–8.

Puddings, Steamed Many excellent ones are available ready to heat up and serve. Alternatively, use a packet of ready-mix pudding; see page 184. Any of these can become your own speciality by the choice of sauce and accompaniments.

Purées Many fruits can be bought in pulp form, sold for pie fillings. Alternatively, make a quick one by putting drained canned fruit in the electric blender for a few seconds. Canned vegetables are pulped in the same way.

Rice and Rolled Oats Always buy the quick cooking varieties.

Roux Always keep some ready-made in the refrigerator or freezer for making quick sauces and thickening other liquids; see page 54.

Sauces Make quick ones by thickening hot liquids with ready-made roux or use one-stage method page 54. Alternatively, use canned or packet sauces or canned cream soups. Use canned curry paste for curries and curry sauces. See also pages 55–64.

Stock Use chicken or beef cubes, meat extracts and vegetable extracts. For better quality dishes use canned consommé in place of stock. Canned vegetable juices and tomato juice and liquor from canned vegetables are also suitable. Use any of these in recipes calling for stock and use them to blend with canned and packet soups to give variety and increase the yield.

Vegetables When prepared vegetables are a recipe ingredient and there is no time to prepare from raw use dehydrated, dried, or deep frozen ones. In salads and for garnishing, use canned ones.

CHAPTER SIX

Appetisers and Hors d'Oeuvre

STORES LIST

Keep a selection of these in the store cupboard for making a quick first course:

Anchovy Fillets These can be bought in very small cans. Serve them plain or use them to garnish egg, potato or Russian salad.

Artichoke Hearts These are sold canned. Drain, rinse, drain again and dress with French dressing.

Asparagus Either canned tips or frozen. Cook the latter, cool and dress with French dressing. Drain the canned tips and serve plain or with dressing.

Beans, Baked Use canned ones, served cold.

Beans, Butter Use canned ones, drain, dress with French dressing and sprinkle with chopped parsley or chives.

Beans, French Cook frozen ones, drain, cool and dress with French dressing; sprinkle with a little chopped onion or hard-boiled egg. Drain canned ones and use in the same way.

Beetroot Either pickled beetroot used as it is with a little grated horseradish sprinkled over, or use canned beets and dress them with vinegar or French dressing.

Cod's Roe, Smoked Usually canned and best served with thin, hot toast as a first course by itself. Serve pieces of lemon with it.
    Alternatively, spread it on small pieces of rye bread and serve as part of the hors d'oeuvre.

Crab Serve canned crab with a little French dressing or mayonnaise, or use it to make a fish cocktail.

Eggs Always keep some hard-boiled ones in the refrigerator where they will keep fresh for a week at least. Use them for garnishing other foods or by themselves with mayonnaise and a garnish of anchovies or sweet peppers.

Gherkins These can be the very small ones sold in jars. Serve plain or use to garnish other dishes. Or keep some cans of the large sweet pickled ones and serve them whole or sliced.

Herrings Many different kinds of canned herrings are available. Especially suitable for hors d'oeuvre are the Scandinavian ones, usually in a sauce. Serve straight from the can. Roll mops (raw pickled herring) are sold in small jars and keep well in a cool place. Serve just one with a little salad as a dish on its own or cut them into pieces and serve as a part of a mixed hors d'oeuvre.

Horseradish Sauce Sold in small jars. Use with fish and meat.

Lobster In cans. Serve with mayonnaise or French dressing or use to make a fish cocktail; see page 86.

Mayonnaise Always keep some in stock for dressing eggs and other foods. Your own make will keep in a cool place but not in the refrigerator.

Mushrooms Canned ones, drain and dress with French dressing and a little finely chopped onion and parsley.

Mussels Sold in jars or cans. Drain and dress with lemon juice and chopped parsley.

Olives Green olives, plain or stuffed, are sold in jars. Black olives are usually sold loose but will keep well in a polythene bag in the refrigerator.

Onions Choose from small white cocktail onions, pickled onions or canned French fried onions; or use fresh sliced or chopped onions with other foods.

Oysters Fresh ones served as a separate dish with lemon and brown bread and butter. Canned ones drained and dressed with lemon and chopped parsley, or use them to make a fish cocktail; see page 86.

Pâté Sold in small cans in a variety of flavours: liver, smoked salmon, smoked trout, grouse, prawn, smoked goose and others. Usually served by themselves with thin hot toast or they may be spread on small squares of bread and served with other foods.

Peppers, Red Sweet Sold in small cans. Drain and serve as they are or mix them with sliced tomatoes and French dressing, or use them to garnish other foods.

Potatoes Available as canned potato salad, or packets of crisps or sticks.

Prawns Canned ones are usually better than frozen. Use them plain with lemon or to garnish other foods, or make a fish cocktail; see page 86.

Red Cabbage, Pickled Available in jars. Serve plain.

Russian Salad Available in cans. Serve plain.

Sardines Canned ones, usually served plain.

Shrimps Either canned or frozen. Serve plain or use to make a fish cocktail; see page 86. Potted shrimps are an hors d'oeuvre on their own with brown bread and butter and wedges of lemon.

Tomatoes Keep some in the refrigerator in a covered dish. Slice and dress with French dressing (plus a pinch of sugar) and garnish with chopped parsley or tarragon.

Tongue Slice canned tongue, dress with French dressing and chopped parsley or serve plain.

Walnuts Pickled ones in jars. Serve plain.

OTHER HORS D'OEUVRE NEEDING LITTLE PREPARATION

Avocado Pear Cut in half, remove stone and fill centre with French dressing.

Buckling Small smoked fish sold ready to eat. Serve with lemon wedges.

Eel Sold as jellied eels or smoked; the latter is sliced thinly and served with lemon wedges.

Mackerel, Smoked Serve with wedges of lemon or with horse-radish sauce.

Melon Chilled slices served by themselves or with cold ham.

Salmon, Smoked Serve with wedges of lemon and brown bread and butter.

Sausages Slices of liver, garlic, salami or other cooked sausage. Serve plain or with young radishes.

Sprats, Smoked Serve with wedges of lemon and brown bread and butter.

Trout, Smoked Serve with horseradish sauce.

CHAPTER SEVEN

Quick Soups with an Individual Touch

BELOW is a list showing the wide variety of canned and packet soups available. The quality varies considerably so experiment to find the ones you like. Then give them an individual touch by adding, e.g., cream, fresh or soured, youghurt, evaporated milk, beaten egg, wine, sherry or marsala, fresh chopped herbs, bottled sauces and ketchup, chopped mushrooms, shredded Brussels sprouts, grated carrots, grated cheese, pasta, rice, rolled oats. Or try mixing two different kinds or using consommé, soup cubes, tomato juice or vegetable juices to dilute concentrated ones instead of water.

Many canned and packet soups make excellent cold ones for hot weather; see pages 48, 51 and 52.

Varieties of Ready-prepared Soups

Asparagus, (usually cream of)	Minestrone
Bean with Bacon	Mulligatawny
Beef Broth	Mushroom
Bisque d'Homard	Onion

Bouillabaisse
Celery
Chicken Broth
Cream of Chicken
Chicken Gumbo
Chicken Noodle
Chicken and Rice
Clam Chowder
Chinese Bird's Nest
Cock-a-leekie
Consommé
Game
Kangaroo Tail
Kidney
Leek
Leek and Potato
Lentil
Lobster

Oxtail
Paprika Goulash
Pea, Green
Pea and Ham
Pea, Spanish
Petite Marmite
Pheasant
Scotch Broth
Sharks' Fins
Scampi Bisque
Tomato
Tomato and Rice
Turkey
Turtle
Vegetable
Vichyssoise
Wild Duck

Quick Garnishes

Brussels sprouts, sliced raw
Cheese, grated
Chives, chopped or scissor
   snipped
Cornflakes
Carrot, raw grated
Cream, seasoned whipped
Cucumber, sliced
Lemon, sliced

Onion, dehydrated
Olives, sliced stuffed
Orange rind, grated
Parsley, chopped or scissor
   snipped
Pasta, garnishing
Radishes, sliced
Sausage, sliced Frankfurters or
   smoked

CREAM SOUPS IN THE ELECTRIC BLENDER. These are quickly made from canned vegetables. As they have no flour thickening, they are thinner than ready-made cream soups and usually have a better flavour.

COOKING TIME: 3–4 mins: QUANTITIES for 4–6

12–15 oz can of vegetables (375–450 g)

Empty the contents of the can into the blender goblet, mix until smooth and then pour into a saucepan.

½ pt milk (1 c or ¼ l): ½ pt water (1 c or ¼ l): 1 chicken cube: salt and pepper: pinch of mace, nutmeg or other flavouring

Add to the pan and bring to the boil, stirring frequently.

4 Tbs evaporated milk or single cream

Add just before serving.

SUITABLE VEGETABLES Asparagus, carrot, garden peas, artichoke hearts, celery, broad beans.

OYSTER SOUP

COOKING TIME: 10 mins: QUANTITIES for 4

8 oz can of oysters (250 g)

Open can and drain the oysters, keeping the stock.

Milk to make stock up to 1 pt (2 c or ½ l): 1 oz roux (30 g)

Heat the milk and stock and, when hot, add the ready-prepared roux and stir until it thickens and boils. Add the oysters and simmer for a few minutes.

Pinch of ground mace or nutmeg: salt and pepper: lemon juice: chopped parsley

Add these to taste and serve.

USING CANNED CONSOMMÉ

CONSOMMÉ WITH EGG AND SHERRY

COOKING TIME: A few minutes: QUANTITIES for 4–6

1 ½ pt consommé (3 c or 2 cans or ¾ l): 4 eggs: 1 Tbs sherry

Heat the consommé to boiling point, remove from the heat, add the unbeaten eggs and sherry and beat well, using a rotary or electric beater. Serve at once in soup cups or bowls.

JELLIED CONSOMMÉ. Put unopened cans of consommé in the refrigerator for 24 hrs. To serve, spoon the jelly into small dishes breaking it up or chopping it. If it is wanted in a hurry, pour the consommé into freezing trays and put in the ice-making compartment of the refrigerator just until it is set.

CONSOMMÉ WITH PASTA. Heat the consommé and cook small decorative pasta in it or use vermicelli.

CONSOMMÉ WITH SHERRY OR WINE. Heat the consommé and, just before serving, add wine or sherry to taste; about 1 Tbs per portion. Serve with toast.

QUICK CHICKEN SOUP

COOKING TIME: ½ hr: QUANTITIES for 4

1 *chicken carcase (remains of boiled or roast chicken): 2 pt water (4 c or 1 l): 6 peppercorns: 1 stick celery, sliced: 1 onion, peeled: 1 carrot, sliced: 1 tsp salt.*

Cook these together in a pressure cooker for about 20 mins. Strain and return the stock to the pan.

White roux

Drop in pieces of white roux and cook and stir until it thickens and boils.

Few sliced mushrooms or stalks: few shredded Brussels sprouts

Add to the soup and boil for a few minutes. Taste for seasoning.

2 Tbs cream

Stir in just before serving.

CHICKEN AND LEEK SOUP

COOKING TIME: 20–30 mins: QUANTITIES for 4

3 leeks

Wash and slice.

1 *chicken cube 1½ pt water (3 c or ¾ l) or, omit cube and use chicken stock*

Bring water and cube or stock to the boil.

1 Tbs rolled oats

Sprinkle into the stock and add the leeks. Cover and boil gently until the leeks are quite tender.

Salt and pepper

Season the soup well.

Grated cheese

Hand separately to be sprinkled on at table.

ALMOND SOUP

COOKING TIME: 15 mins: QUANTITIES for 4

8 oz blanched almonds (250 g): 1 ½ pt chicken stock (3 c or ¾ l): 1 small onion

Peel the onion and put almonds and onion in the blender with a little of the stock to moisten. Blend until smooth. Put in a pan with the rest of the stock and simmer for 15 mins.

4 Tbs evaporated milk or single cream: Milk if needed

Add evaporated milk or cream to the soup and thin with ordinary milk if necessary. Serve hot.

LENTIL SOUP. Quick to prepare and leave to cook in a slow oven with other dishes. Then refrigerate and use later on.

COOKING TIME: 1–2 hrs: QUANTITIES for 4–5

1 carrot: 1 onion: 1 stick of celery: 1 small turnip

Peel these and put through a coarse shredder. Put in a pan with:

7 oz lentils (¾ c or 200 g): pinch dried herbs: pepper: 4 rashers streaky bacon cut in small pieces: 1 beef cube: 2 pt water (4 c or 1 l)

Cook slowly until the lentils are tender, the exact time is not important. Cooking can be in a casserole in the oven or on a low heat on top. If not required for service at once, cool the soup and put in a covered bowl in the refrigerator.

When required thin with:

Milk to give desired thickness and a little cream if liked

Heat to boiling, taste for seasoning. Sprinkle with:

Chopped parsley

Serve hot.

COLD CURRIED CHICKEN SOUP

QUANTITIES for 4

*2 cans (1 pt or ½ l) of condensed cream of chicken soup: 1
pt milk (½ l) or the equivalent of the two cans of soup: 1 tsp
curry powder*

Chill the soup in the refrigerator for several hours. Open the cans
and turn the soup into a bowl. Add chilled milk equal to the soup
in volume. Add it gradually, stirring and beating to blend well. Beat
in the curry powder. Serve at once or return to the refrigerator to
keep cold. Serve in soup cups or cereal bowls.

Chopped spring onion or parsley

Sprinkle a little in the centre of each portion.

CHEESE SOUP

COOKING TIME: 10–15 mins: QUANTITIES for 3–4

*2 oz dried milk powder (5 Tbs or 60 g): 1 tsp cornflour: ½ tsp
dry mustard: 1 pt warm water (2 c or ½ l)*

Put these in the blender and mix until smooth. Pour into a saucepan, bring to the boil, stirring frequently, and simmer for 5 mins.

*2 oz butter or margarine (4 Tbs or 60 g): salt and pepper: 2 oz
processed cheddar cheese (2 slices or 60 g)*

Add to the pan and heat, without boiling until the cheese is melted.
Season to taste.

1 oz chopped watercress or lettuce (1 c or 30 g)
Add to the soup and serve.

ICED SWEET PEPPER SOUP

QUANTITIES for 4

8 oz can of red pimentos (250 g): 1 pt canned tomato juice (2 c or ½ l)

Drain the pimentos and put them in the electric blender. Add the tomato juice and blend until smooth.

Salt and sugar

Add these to taste and then chill thoroughly.

Parsley or other green herbs

Serve the chilled soup in bowls with a green garnish.

CHAPTER EIGHT

Good Quick Sauces

THERE are some good ready-prepared sauces to be had, though quality varies and the good ones are sometimes hard to find. Best places to look are in big stores and delicatessens. Many are available from mail order firms.

Ready-prepared sauces include:

Sauce Abricoma (Apricot)
Sauce Alexandra (Wild strawberry)
Apple Sauce
Sauce Bearnaise
Blue Cheese dressing
Bread Sauce
Camembert Sauce
Cheese Sauce
Chilli Sauce
Cole Slaw dressing
Cranberry Sauce
Cumberland Sauce

Ketchups, various
Lobster Sauce
Madeira Wine Sauce
Mayonnaise, various
Sauce Melba
Mint Sauce
Mushroom Sauce
Newburg Sauce
Onion Sauce
Sauce Robert
Salad Cream, various
Sanfayna (Tomato and Sweet Pepper)

Curry Sauce

Sauce Diable

French dressing

Horseradish Sauce

Soy Sauce

Tartare Sauce

White Sauce

TWO QUICK METHODS OF MAKING BASIC SAUCES

1. ROUX METHOD. A roux is the basic thickening for many sauces. Instead of making a little for each sauce, make the following bulk recipe which will keep several weeks in the refrigerator and longer in the freezer.

Weigh it out into 1 or 2 oz portions (30 or 60 g). Wrap individually in foil and put the portions in a polythene bag in the refrigerator or in the freezer.

To thicken sauces, stews, gravies, etc., simply drop pieces of the roux in the hot liquid and stir until it thickens and boils.

8 oz butter (1 c or 250 g): 8 oz plain flour (1 ½ c or 250 g)

Melt the butter and stir in the flour. Cook gently for a few minutes to make a 'white' roux, suitable for most sauces. If a brown roux is wanted for brown sauces and gravies, cook very slowly until the mixture turns a light brown. This is best done in a wide pan or tin in a moderate oven.

QUANTITIES to use for thickening:

Thin sauce—2 oz (60 g) roux to 1 pint (½ l) liquid: medium sauce—3 oz (100 g) roux to 1 pint (½ l) liquid: thick sauce—4 oz (120 g) roux to 1 pint (1 ½ l) liquid

2. ONE-STAGE METHOD

QUANTITIES for 1 pt liquid (½ l)

Basic sauce.

1 ½ oz butter or margarine (3 Tbs or 45 g): 1 ½ oz flour (4 ½ Tbs or 45 g)

Thin Sauce. Make above mixture and thin as desired.

Thick Sauce.

2 oz butter or margarine (4 Tbs or 60 g): 2 oz flour (6 Tbs or 60 g)

The fat should be soft and at room temperature. If it comes straight out of the refrigerator, cut it in pieces and warm in the pan before adding the other ingredients. Add flour and liquid and heat and beat with a rotary beater, hand or electric, until the sauce boils. Continue beating and heating for 2–3 minutes. Add flavourings to taste. Any recipe using fat, flour and liquid can be made this way, adding the flavourings after the sauce has cooked. Unless you have a non-stick pan it is wise to cook over a moderate heat or the sauce may stick.

ANCHOVY SAUCE

QUANTITIES: for 4

1 *pt white sauce (2 c or ½ l) see page 63: pepper: 2 tsp anchovy essence: chopped capers (optional)*

Add these to the hot sauce and serve hot.

APPLE SAUCE

COOKING TIME: ½ hr without attention: QUANTITIES for 4

1 *lb cooking apples (½ kg): 2 oz sugar (¼ c or 60 g)*

Wash the apples and cut them up roughly. Cook in a saucepan with just enough water to prevent burning, or alternatively, cook them in a covered dish in the oven. When pulpy put through a sieve. Re-heat with the sugar.

Alternatively, use peeled and cored apples, fresh or frozen, and simply cook to a pulp with the sugar and minimum water.

Prepared apple sauce deep freezes very well. Re-heat it in a double boiler or in a covered dish in the oven.

Basting sauces for grilled meat, fish and poultry

OIL AND VERMOUTH (for chicken or veal)

QUANTITIES for 4

⅛ *pt oil (¼ c or ¾ dl): ⅛ pt dry Vermouth (¼ c or ¾ dl): ½ tsp salt: pinch of pepper*

Mix thoroughly before use and brush over the food several times during cooking.

BASIC BARBECUE SAUCE

> 1 *tsp dry mustard:* 2 *tsp Worcester sauce:* 2 *Tbs vinegar:* 3 *Tbs oil or melted butter*

Mix together and use to baste the food several times during grilling.

OPTIONAL EXTRAS: *chopped herbs or crushed garlic*

MARINADE AND BASTING SAUCE

> ¼ *pt red or white wine* (½ *c or* 1½ *dl*): ¼ *pt oil* (½ *c or* 1½ *dl*): 1 *small bayleaf:* ½ *tsp chopped fresh herbs:* 1 *clove garlic*

Crush the garlic and add the other ingredients. To marinate food put it in a shallow dish and pour the mixture over it. Cover and store in the refrigerator for 1 hour or longer. Use the marinade for basting during cooking.

FISH BASTING SAUCE see page 82.

BÉCHAMEL SAUCE. This can be made in advance and stored in the refrigerator or in the freezer, so when you want some make more than enough for one meal and store the rest.

COOKING TIME: 15–20 mins: QUANTITIES for 8

> 1 *pt milk* (2 *c or* ½ *l*): 1 *shallot or onion: piece of carrot: piece of celery:* 1 *bay leaf:* 10 *peppercorns*

Peel the onion or shallot and clean the other vegetables. Put all the ingredients in a pan and bring to the boil. Remove from the heat, cover and leave to infuse for a minimum of 5 mins. Then strain and return to the pan.

> 2–4 *oz prepared roux* (60–125 *g*) (*see page* 54): 4 *Tbs single cream: salt*

Use the roux to thicken the milk to the desired consistency. Boil for a few minutes. Add salt to taste and the cream just before serving. If it is to be stored for future use it is better not to add the cream until the sauce is re-heated for serving.

BROWN BUTTER SAUCE (for fish, eggs, cauliflower and other vegetables)

COOKING TIME: a few minutes: QUANTITIES for 4
2–4 oz butter (4–8 Tbs or 60–125 g)

Heat in a small pan until the butter turns nut brown.

1–2 tsp chopped parsley: 1–2 tsp vinegar

Add parsley and cook for a few seconds, then add the vinegar and pour the sauce quickly over the food.

CAPER SAUCE

QUANTITIES for 4

1 pt fish or meat stock (2 c or ½ l): 3 oz roux (100 g)

Heat the stock and add the roux, stirring until it thickens, or use one-stage method, page 54.

2 Tbs chopped capers: 1½ Tbs vinegar from the capers: salt and pepper to taste

Add these to the sauce and serve hot.

CARAMEL SAUCE (for puddings and fruit)

COOKING TIME: 5 mins: QUANTITIES for 4

4 oz sugar (½ c or 125 g): ⅛ pt water (¼ c or ¾ dl)

Heat these together in a small pan until the sugar dissolves. Boil hard, without stirring, until the mixture turns amber coloured. Remove the pan from the heat and allow to cool a little.

⅛ pt water (¼ c or ¾ dl)

Add to the caramel and heat and stir until it all dissolves. Serve hot or cold.

CELERY SAUCE (for boiled meat or poultry)

QUANTITIES for 4–6

1 *lb can celery* (½ *kg*): *evaporated milk*: *salt and pepper*: *ground mace or onion powder*

Empty the contents of the can of celery into the goblet of the electric blender. Mix until smooth. Turn into a saucepan and heat, adding evaporated milk to give a creamy consistency. Season to taste and serve hot.

QUICK CHEESE SAUCE

¼ *pt evaporated milk* (½ *c or* 1½ *dl*): 4 *oz processed cheese* (125 *g*): *a little French mustard*: *salt and pepper to taste*: *wine* (*optional*)

Chop the cheese roughly and put all the ingredients into a saucepan. Heat gently until the cheese melts and the sauce thickens. Add seasoning to taste and serve at once.

ALTERNATIVES: If a thicker sauce is required, add:

1 *egg* (*beaten*)

and allow to cook, without boiling.

QUICK CHOCOLATE SAUCE No.1

QUANTITIES for 4

4 *oz plain chocolate* (125 *g*)

Break the chocolate in pieces and melt it gently over a pan of hot water.

¼ *pt evaporated milk, undiluted* (½ *c or* 1½ *dl*)

Add to chocolate and mix and heat until smooth

Vanilla, rum, brandy or liqueur to taste

Flavour to taste and serve hot or cold. If necessary, thin with a little more milk or cream.

QUICK CHOCOLATE SAUCE No. 2

QUANTITIES for 4

3 oz drinking chocolate powder (½ c or 1 ½ dl): 2 Tbs water

Mix these in a small pan and bring to the boil, stirring all the time.

1 tsp vanilla: top of the milk, or thin cream, or evaporated milk

Add vanilla and dilute to the desired thickness with milk or cream. Serve hot or cold.

EGG AND CURRY SAUCE (for fish and vegetables)

QUANTITIES for 4

2 eggs

Hard boil, shell and mash or chop

4 oz butter (½ c or 125 g): ½ tsp curry powder: ¼ tsp paprika pepper

Melt the butter and add the egg and flavourings. Mix well and make sure it is hot before serving. Specially good as a sauce for grilled, steamed or baked fish or with cauliflower.

FISH COCKTAIL SAUCE see page 86.

FRENCH DRESSING see page 63.

FRESH FRUIT SAUCE

QUANTITIES for 4

8 oz fresh ripe or defrosted frozen fruit (250 g): sugar to taste

Put these in the electric blender and mix until smooth. If necessary add a little water, lemon, orange or other juice to dilute to the desired consistency. Suitable for raspberries (use in place of Melba Sauce), strawberries, apricots, blackberries, red currants, cherries and very ripe loganberries. Also suitable for freezing.

It can also be made with canned fruit, using as much of the syrup as necessary to give the desired consistency.

GOOSEBERRY SAUCE (for fish or poultry)

COOKING TIME: 10–20 mins: QUANTITIES for 4

1 lb green gooseberries, fresh or frozen (½ kg): pinch of grated nutmeg: soft brown sugar to taste

Cook the fruit gently in a pan with just enough water to prevent burning. This may be done in a covered dish in the oven. When the fruit is tender, mash well or put in the electric blender or through a mechanical sieve. Add nutmeg and sugar to taste.

A small knob of butter

Add just before serving and serve hot.

MAKING GRAVY

Thin Gravy Remove the meat to a hot dish. Tilt the roasting pan to make the drippings flow down to one corner. Wait a few moments for the sediment to settle and then pour off the fat very gently leaving the juices behind. Add stock to the pan and stir to dissolve all the sediment. If the pan is a suitable one, put it on the hotplate and bring the gravy to the boil, stirring frequently. Alternatively, pour the gravy into a small saucepan and heat it in this. Season to taste and add a little wine, cider or stout, as desired. Strain into a hot gravy boat.

Thick Gravy Thicken the hot gravy made as above either with a little blended cornflour or potato flour (I Tbs to ½ pt or ¼ l) or thicken with roux.

QUICK HOLLANDAISE SAUCE (for fish or vegetables)

¼ pt tepid water (½ c or 1½ dl): 1 oz melted butter (2 Tbs or 30 g): 3 egg yolks: 2 Tbs lemon juice: 2 sprigs parsley: salt and pepper

Put all ingredients in the blender goblet and mix at full speed for 1 minute. Pour into a saucepan and heat gently until it thickens, stirring all the time. Serve at once.

JAM SAUCE

COOKING TIME: 5 mins: QUANTITIES for 4

½ oz cornflour (1½ Tbs or 15 g): 1 pt water (2 c or ½ l)

Blend the cornflour with a little cold water. Heat the remaining water and when it is boiling, pour it into the blended mixture. Return to the pan and stir until it thickens. Boil 5 mins.

4 oz jam (4 Tbs or 125 g): 2 tsp lemon juice

Add these to the sauce and mix well. Serve hot or cold.

MAYONNAISE (in the blender)

1 egg: 2 Tbs lemon juice or vinegar: 1 tsp French mustard: pinch of sugar: pinch of salt

Put these in the goblet of the blender.

¼–½ pt oil (½–1 c or 1½–3 dl)

Set the speed to maximum and add the oil through the hole in the lid. Continue mixing until the mayonnaise is of the desired consistency. It will thicken more when it is removed from the goblet. If a thinner mayonnaise is required, add lemon juice or vinegar.

CURRY MAYONNAISE

½ pt mayonnaise (1 c or ¼ l): 1–2 Tbs curry powder

Blend well and use for vegetable, fish or meat salad.

MELBA SAUCE (see also French Fruit Sauce, page 59)

COOKING TIME: 10–15 mins: QUANTITIES for 4

12 oz fresh or frozen raspberries (375 g)

Cook the fruit, without any water, until it is reduced to a pulp. Sieve.

½ Tbs cornflour or potato flour

Blend flour with a little cold water and stir it into the raspberry pulp. Stir and heat until it thickens.

Sugar: lemon juice

Add these to taste, cool and store in a covered jar in the refrigerator or in the freezer.

QUICK MUSTARD SAUCE (for smoked or fresh fish)

QUANTITIES for 4

2 oz butter (4 Tbs or 60 g): 4 tsp French mustard

Melt these together and stir well before pouring the sauce over the fish.

PARSLEY SAUCE Add 4 Tbs chopped parsley to 1 pt (½ l) white or Béchamel Sauce or use packet sauce.

TARTARE SAUCE

½ pt mayonnaise (1 c or ¼ l): 2 Tbs chopped gherkins or capers 1 tsp finely chopped onion or use dried chopped onion

Mix all together and thin with vinegar or lemon juice if desired. Serve cold.

QUICK TOMATO SAUCE

QUANTITIES for 4

½ pt can condensed tomato soup (¼ l): 1 Tbs tarragon vinegar: 1 tsp brown sugar: 1 Tbs Worcester sauce: salt and pepper

Mix all together, bring to the boil and serve.

VINAIGRETTE SAUCE

4 Tbs salad oil: 2 Tbs tarragon vinegar: 1 tsp each of finely chopped gherkin, shallot and parsley: salt and pepper: ½ tsp French mustard

Mix all the ingredients together and stir before serving.

WHITE SAUCE

Use either Béchamel sauce page 56, or use milk and thicken with roux, see page 54, or use milk and one-stage method page 54.

SALAD DRESSINGS

FRENCH DRESSING

QUANTITIES for 4

1 ½ Tbs olive oil: pinch of pepper: ½ Tbs vinegar (wine, tarragon or other flavour) or 1 Tbs lemon juice: ½ tsp dry mustard: ¼ tsp salt

Mix oil and seasonings and add vinegar or lemon. Stir well before using.

A larger amount may be mixed and stored in a covered jar or bottle. Shake well before using.

SOUR CREAM DRESSING

QUANTITIES for 4

2 hard boiled eggs: 1 tsp salt: ¼ pt sour or cultured cream (½ c or 1 ½ dl): ¼ tsp pepper: 1 tsp dry mustard

Separate the egg yolks from the whites and mash the yolks and seasonings in a small basin. Gradually work in the cream. Use the egg whites to garnish the salad.

MAYONNAISE see page 61.

MUSTARD SALAD DRESSING (for potato salad)

QUANTITIES for 4

2 Tbs dry mustard: 1 Tbs sugar: pinch of salt: pinch of pepper

Combine in a small basin or in the salad bowl and add enough water to mix to a smooth paste.

½ Tbs oil: 1 Tbs vinegar: 1 Tbs single cream

Add to the other ingredients and mix well. Combine gently with the diced potatoes.

YOGHURT SALAD DRESSING

QUANTITIES for 4

1 ½ Tbs lemon juice: ¼ tsp French mustard: ¼ pt yoghurt (1 small jar or 1 ½ dl): pinch of pepper: ¼ tsp salt

Mix lemon juice and seasonings together and slowly stir in the yoghurt. Blend thoroughly and chill for ½ hour before serving.

CHAPTER NINE

Never be without Cheese

CHEESE is invaluable for quick meals and, with the very wide variety of English and imported cheese available there need be no monotony.

Bread and cheese with salad or fruit makes a perfect snack meal. Serve cheese and biscuits or cheese and fruit instead of a sweet course. Use it to make quick cheese sauce for vegetables or fish, see page 58.

Always keep some grated cheese to serve with soup or pasta, as a garnish for vegetables and other savoury dishes, for sandwich fillings and to add to salads. Parmesan cheese is sold ready grated in packets or drums, and some shops sell grated Cheddar.

STORING CHEESE

Wrap it loosely in a polythene bag or tightly in aluminium foil and put it in a cool place or in the refrigerator. Remove from the refrigerator 1 hour before using to allow it to come back to room temperature. Grated cheese can be stored in a glass jar, covered loosely, and in a cool, dry place or in the refrigerator. Shake the jar occasionally. If the cheese is purchased in a box or wrapper, store it in this. Soft cheese (cottage and Camembert) will keep for about a week, others for 2 weeks or more. Camembert, Brie, etc. will keep 6–9 months in the freezer. Defrost 1–2 days in the refrigerator and then serve at room temperature.

COOKING WITH CHEESE

For a good flavour choose a fairly strong cheese. To save time, either use cheese sold ready grated or use processed cheese which can be quickly chopped into small pieces and melted in liquid or sauce. Sliced processed cheese is useful for putting on the top of other food to be melted under the grill or in the oven. It is also useful for toasted sandwiches.

Cheese only needs to melt. If cooked too long at a high temperature it becomes tough and stringy. When making sauces and soups, cook them completely before adding the cheese and then heat just long enough to melt it. If cheese is to be browned under the grill do it for the shortest possible time.

CHEESE AS A SEPARATE COURSE

Provide either one cheese or a selection on a cheese board. Serve with it either bread, rolls, biscuits, toast or rusks. Good cheese requires no butter though some people like it.

Accompaniments can be any of the following: pickles, salad, celery, watercress, radishes, leaves of chicory, carrot sticks, raw fruit (especially apples, pears or grapes) or nuts.

To drink with the cheese beer or red wine are best, or serve cider or chilled milk.

CHEESE WITH SOUP

A very good snack meal for cold days is a bowl of soup with bread and cheese and salad.

Otherwise, either serve grated cheese to sprinkle on at table or put a piece of toast in the bottom of each soup bowl, sprinkle it thickly with cheese and then pour in the hot soup.

CHEESE FOR BREAKFAST

This is one of the best breakfasts that needs no cooking. Use a firm cheese cut in thin slices or use sliced processed cheese. It is usually eaten with a knife and fork like a slice of meat and bread or rolls and butter are eaten with it.

Another good way is to serve Cheddar cheese with marmalade and hot buttered toast or buttered oatcakes.

A slice of toasted bread with a slice of cheese melted on top also makes a quick tasty breakfast. Top this with one or two slices of raw tomato or with half a grilled tomato.

CHEESE SALADS

Cheese goes well with all salad vegetables and crumbled blue vein cheeses are sometimes mixed with a mayonnaise or thick salad dressing. Serve the cheese either in a piece (like meat) to be eaten with the salad, or cut it in cubes and mix it into the salad ingredients; or grate it coarsely and arrange it in heaps in the middle of the salad.

Cottage cheese, and other soft cheeses can be used to stuff tomatoes, cucumber cups or as a filling for hamrolls.

For other Salad recipes, see pages 148–9.

CHEESE CREAMS. To serve as a first course or with salad for a snack meal. Quick and easy to make and will keep several days in the refrigerator.

QUANTITIES for 4

¼ pt whipping cream or chilled evaporated milk (½ c or 1½ dl):
½ tsp salt: Pinch each of pepper and dry mustard

Whip these together until the cream is stiff.

¼ pt just melted aspic jelly, use ready made from a jar or can
(½ c or 1½ dl): 2 oz finely grated Parmesan cheese (½ c or 60 g)

Add these to the cream mixture and pour into four individual (¼ pt) moulds or one large mould. Chill to set, unmould and garnish with:

Salad vegetables

CHEESE CUSTARD

COOKING TIME ½/¾ hr or 3 mins pressure cooking:
QUANTITIES for 4: TEMPERATURE: E 350°F, G 4

Grease 4 individual pudding moulds or cups.

½ pt milk (1 c or ¼ l): ½ oz butter (1 Tbs or 15 g)

Heat these together until the butter melts.

4 eggs: 2 oz grated Parmesan cheese (½ c or 60 g): 1 tsp prepared mustard: pinch each of cayenne and paprika peppers

Beat the eggs to blend whites and yolks. Add the other ingredients. Add the hot milk, mix and pour into the moulds. Cover each with foil and pressure cook (let the pressure reduce slowly), or bake in a pan of water in the oven slowly. Turn out of the moulds and serve hot with toast or cold with salad or by itself for a light supper dish or first course.

CHEESE FONDUE

QUANTITIES for 4

A cut clove of garlic

Rub the fondue dish with this.

⅛ pt white wine (¼ c or ¾ dl)

Add to the dish and allow to warm.

4 oz Gruyère or Emmenthal cheese, coarsely grated (125 g)

Add to the wine and heat until the cheese melts, stirring all the time.

1 Tbs Kirsch or dry sherry

Add to the fondue and cook until it thickens. Put on the table over the spirit lamp.

Pieces of bread

Serve these separately for the diners to spear on forks and dip into the central dish of fondue.

ALTERNATIVE: Buy ready-prepared fondue for melting.

WELSH RAREBIT

COOKING TIME about 15 mins: QUANTITIES for 4

1 oz butter or margarine (2 Tbs or 30 g)

Heat in a small pan until melted

4 Tbs milk, ale or stout: 2 tsp made mustard or Worcester sauce: 8 oz grated Cheddar or Cheshire cheese (2 c) or 8 oz sliced processed cheese

If processed cheese is used, break or chop it into small pieces. Put all ingredients in the pan, heat gently stirring frequently until smooth and creamy. Avoid heating too fast or the cheese will go stringy.

4 slices toast

Spread the mixture on the hot toast and brown under the grill.

BUCK RAREBIT

Serve a poached egg on top of each portion of Welsh rarebit.

CHAPTER TEN

Take some Eggs

MOST savoury egg dishes are quickly prepared and cooked. Keep plenty of fresh eggs in stock and some hard-boiled ones too. Keep them in the refrigerator and they will be useful for making quick snacks, for eating plain with bread and butter, to make salads, for garnishing and for sandwich fillings. Next time you boil some for breakfast put in some extra and leave them to boil hard after the breakfast ones have been served.

BEATING EGGS. They beat to a larger volume more quickly if they are at room temperature. If taken straight from the refrigerator, break them into the basin and then stand this in warm water for a few minutes to take the chill off. Beating is easier and the results better if the eggs are a few days old and egg whites beat up better if they are beginning to go watery.

For just one or two eggs to be added to sauces, soups and so on, use a small whisk made of spiral wire or one of the balloon type.

For larger quantities and when thorough beating is needed, use an electric egg beater. Choose a bowl small enough for the beaters to be covered by the unbeaten egg to at least half their depth, otherwise they will take a long time to beat.

STORING EGGS See page 25.

BACON AND EGGS—FRIED. Remove the rinds and place the rashers in a cold pan, overlapping with the fat sides touching the bottom of the pan. Cook slowly for 6–8 mins turning occasionally and, if crisp bacon is liked, keep pouring the fat off. Do not fry the bacon too quickly as this makes it frizzle and become hard. Remove the cooked bacon to a hot dish.

Crack the eggs separately into a cup and slide each into the hot fat, turn down the heat and cook gently 2–3 mins, or until they are set. Cooking too fast makes the whites tough and unappetising. Lift the eggs out of the pan, using a fish slice and serve with the bacon.

BACON AND EGGS—GRILLED. Remove rinds and place bacon on the grill rack. Cook under a moderate heat, or some distance from the heat. Cook two minutes each side or until done to taste. Remove and keep hot.

Lift out the grill rack and crack an egg into a saucer. Slide it into the fat at the bottom of the grill pan. If you are not doing enough eggs to fill the grill pan, tilt it to begin the cooking and then right it when the eggs have begun to set. Lift the eggs out with a slice.

BACON AND EGGS IN THE OVEN. This way needs least attention of all and is suitable for the auto-timer.

Grease a fireproof dish or tin. Remove rinds from bacon and place the rashers in the bottom of the dish. Crack the eggs into a saucer and put into the dish on top of the bacon. Chipolata sausages and halved tomatoes may also be added. If mushrooms are wanted, put a knob of butter in the cup of each.

Bake at E 375°F, G 5: for about 30 mins or until the eggs are set.

BAKED EGGS RAYMOND

COOKING TIME: 10–15 mins: QUANTITIES for 4
TEMPERATURE: E 375°, G 5

1 oz butter (2 Tbs or 30 g)

Melt this in a flat baking dish.

4 Tbs canned shrimps: 4 Tbs double cream

Rinse and drain the shrimps. Scatter them over the bottom of the dish and pour in the cream.

1–2 eggs per person: Salt and pepper

Break the eggs separately into a saucer and slide into the baking dish. Season with salt and pepper.

2–4 oz grated Parmesan or Cheddar cheese (½–1 c or 60–125g)

Sprinkle a layer of cheese over the eggs and bake in a moderate oven until the eggs are set. Brown the top under the grill.

BAKED SPAGHETTI AND EGG. See page 182.

BOILING EGGS

COOKING TIMES:

Soft-Boiled (soft whites, liquid yolks)
Large 3 mins, Standard 2¾ mins, Medium 2½ mins
Medium-Boiled (firm whites, soft yolks)
Large 4½ mins, Standard 4 mins, Medium 3½ mins
Hard-Boiled (firm whites and yolks)
Large 8–10 mins, Standard 7 mins, Medium 6 mins

If the eggs have come straight out of the refrigerator, hold them under the hot tap a few minutes before cooking. This will help to prevent the shells from cracking during boiling. Hard-boiled eggs to be served cold should be plunged into cold water as soon as they are cooked. Over-cooking produces a dark band between yolk and white.

Method 1. Put the eggs into cold water to cover. Bring to the boil, turn down the heat to simmering and cook for the desired time. Do not use a lid. Count the time from boiling point.

Method 2 (for an electric hotplate). Put the eggs in a single layer in a pan with 3–4 Tbs water. Put on the lid and heat until the water boils. Turn off the heat and count the time from then.

CODDLED EGGS. These take a little longer than boiling but are more tender to eat.

   COOKING TIME for medium done: Large 8–9 mins, Standard 8 mins, Medium 7 mins, *Hard-Boiled* about 20 mins

Heat enough water to cover the eggs to the depth of about an inch. Bring the water to the boil and use a spoon to lower the eggs gently into it. Put on the lid, remove pan from heat and leave for the required time.

CURRIED EGGS WITH RICE

   COOKING TIME 15 mins: QUANTITIES for 4
   4–8 *eggs*

Put the eggs on to boil for 8–10 mins.

   4–8 *oz rice* (½–1 *c or* 125–250 *g*): ½–1 *pt water* (1–2 *c or* ¼–½ *l*):
   ½–1 *tsp salt*

Put in a pan and bring to the boil, stir once, reduce the heat and cook gently until all the water is absorbed.

   8 *oz canned curry sauce or paste* (250 *g*)

Heat the sauce and, when the eggs are hard-boiled, shell them and add to the sauce, either whole or cut in halves lengthwise. Fluff up the rice with a fork and serve the eggs in a border of the rice.

FRIED EGGS WITH BROWN BUTTER SAUCE

   COOKING TIME: 3–4 mins: QUANTITIES for 4

   1 *oz butter* (2 *Tbs or* 30 *g*)

Put in a frying pan and heat until the butter turns nut brown.

4 *eggs: salt and pepper*

Break the eggs into the hot butter and season each with a pinch of salt and pepper. Cook until the whites are firm. Remove to a hot dish.

1 *Tbs vinegar*

Add vinegar to the pan, mix with remaining butter and pour over the eggs. Serve at once with:

Fingers of toast or fresh rolls

EGGS LYONNAISE. This is a simple dish which can be time-consuming to make but if packet onion sauce and ready-grated cheese are used it can be made in a very short time.

COOKING TIME: 15 mins: QUANTITIES for 2–4

4 *eggs: grated Cheddar or Parmesan cheese or slices of processed cheese:* ½ *pt onion sauce (1 c or ¼ l)*

Hard boil the eggs for 8–10 mins and make the sauce. Cut the eggs in half lengthwise and put them in a fireproof dish. Pour the sauce over them and sprinkle the top thickly with the grated cheese or put slices of processed cheese on top. Heat under the grill until the cheese melts and begins to brown. Serve with bread or toast.

FRENCH OMELET

COOKING TIME: about 2 mins: QUANTITIES for 4

8 *eggs: pinch of pepper,* 1 *tsp salt*

Beat the eggs just enough to mix yolks and whites thoroughly. Add the seasoning.

1 *oz butter (2 Tbs or* 30 *g)*

If the omelets are being cooked singly, use a quarter of the butter for each. There should be enough to grease the bottom of the pan. Heat the butter and when it just begins to change colour, pour in the eggs. Keep a good heat under the pan and use a palette knife to lift the edges as the egg sets and let the uncooked mixture run underneath. When all the egg is cooked, but still moist on top, fold it over away from the handle and tip out onto a hot dish. Serve at once.

VARIATIONS

1. Ham omelet. Add 1 *Tbs chopped parsley and 2 oz chopped lean ham* (60 g) to the eggs before making the omelet.

2. Cheese omelet. Add 2 *oz grated Cheddar cheese* (60 g) *or 1 oz Parmesan cheese* (30 g) to the egg mixture before making the omelet.

SPANISH OMELET

COOKING TIME about 5 mins: QUANTITIES for 4

8 *oz can macedoine* (250 g) *or mixed diced vegetables plus a little canned sweet pepper: 1 oz fat* (2 Tbs or 30 g)

Drain the vegetables thoroughly. Heat the fat in a large frying pan and toss the vegetables in it.

6 *eggs: 1 tsp salt: pinch of pepper: 2 Tbs chopped parsley or chives*

Beat the eggs and add the other ingredients. Pour this over the hot vegetables and cook, without stirring, until the egg is brown underneath. Place in the oven or under the grill to set the top lightly. Fold over or cut in portions and serve at once.

POACHED EGGS

COOKING TIME: 3–5 mins

Only fresh eggs are suitable. Stale ones will not keep a good shape. Put 2 inches water in a frying pan or shallow stew pan. Bring the water to the boil and remove pan from heat. Break the eggs into a saucer and slide them gently into the water. Cover the pan but do not allow the water to boil again. Leave until the whites are lightly set.

Lift out the eggs with a fish slice, rest the slice on a clean cloth to drain and then slide the egg onto a piece of hot buttered toast. Serve at once.

ALTERNATIVE METHOD. Use egg poaching moulds but remember they take longer to wash than a pan.

POACHED EGGS MORNAY

COOKING TIME: 15–20 mins: QUANTITIES for 4

½ pt cheese sauce (1 c or ¼ l), canned or quick recipe: see page 58. 4 poached eggs

Poach the eggs very lightly and then place them in a shallow fire-proof dish, seasoning to taste. Alternatively, place in individual dishes such as heat resistant glass scallop shells. Pour the hot sauce over them and either brown under the grill or in the top of a hot oven. Do this quickly and the eggs should not be hard cooked.

EGG SALAD. See pages 142–52.

EGG SANDWICHES. See pages 202–3.

SCRAMBLED EGGS

COOKING TIME: 5 mins: QUANTITIES for 4

4–5 eggs: ½ tsp salt: pinch of pepper: 6 Tbs milk

Beat the eggs just enough to blend yolks and whites. Add seasoning and milk.

1 oz butter (2 Tbs or 30 g)

Melt the butter in a small pan, preferably a non-stick one. Add the egg mixture being careful not to have the butter too hot. Cook over a very low heat and stir only once or twice during cooking so that the egg sets in big soft clots. Serve as soon as it is set.

4 slices buttered toast

Serve on the toast or serve the toast fingers separately.

VARIATIONS

1. Scrambled egg with bacon. Remove rind from a rasher of bacon and snip it into pieces using kitchen scissors. Fry bacon in the butter before adding the eggs.

2. Scrambled egg with cheese. Add 1 *oz grated cheese (4 Tbs) and 1 Tbs chopped parsley or other green herbs* to the eggs before scrambling.

EGGS IN TOMATO SAUCE

COOKING TIME 10 mins: QUANTITIES for 2–4

4 hard-boiled eggs: ½ pt quick tomato sauce (½ l) see page 62.

Cut the hot, shelled eggs in half lengthwise, or use a slicer. Put them in a hot dish and pour the sauce over them. Serve hot.

CHAPTER ELEVEN

Fish Cooks Quickly

EVEN if you are not able to buy fresh fish easily there are many varieties of frozen fish which are very good as well as a wide variety of canned and smoked fish (see list below). See pages 25 and 34–5 for tips on buying and storing fresh fish.

VARIETIES OF CANNED, FROZEN AND SMOKED FISH AVAILABLE

Anchovy fillets, canned. Used for hors d'oeuvre or to garnish salads or egg dishes, especially good with egg mayonnaise.

Bloaters are salted herrings which have been lightly smoked. They are usually split open and grilled, then served with a pat of butter. They make a good supper dish.

Buckling are smoked herrings which are already cooked and ready for eating cold as hors d'oeuvre, or they may be heated by grilling or frying. Good served with horseradish sauce and boiled potatoes. Also suitable for serving cold as a breakfast fish or for a light meal with salad. Usually sold by delicatessens.

Brisling are very small herrings, smoked and canned in oil or tomato. Suitable for hors d'oeuvre, for snacks on toast or for sandwich fillings or open sandwiches or with salad.

Fish cakes sold ready prepared by the fishmonger or delicatessen or as frozen cakes. Suitable for frying or grilling or baking in a hot oven.

Cod available frozen as fillets or steaks. Some varieties can be sliced and cooked frozen but most are better if de-frosted first. Cod fillets in parsley sauce are available canned. Cod's Roe is sold canned, either fresh or smoked. Fresh cod's roe is sliced and fried. Smoked it is used as hors d'oeuvre on toast or for making sandwiches.

Crab available as frozen dressed crab or canned dressed crab or crab meat. Either served just as dressed crab with lemon and brown bread and butter or used to make a salad or for sandwich fillings.

Eel Jellied eels are sold in jars ready for serving. Smoked eel is sold by delicatessens and is served as hors d'oeuvre, cut in thin slices and accompanied by lemon and brown bread and butter. Also suitable for open sandwiches.

Haddock Sold as smoked haddock, either as fillets or small whole fish; while frozen smoked haddock fillets are sold to cook in a bag with butter. Unsmoked frozen fillets are cooked like fresh haddock.

Herrings Both whole herrings and soft herring roes are deep frozen. Canned herrings are available in a variety of sauces. Canned soft roes are re-heated and served on toast with lemon when they make a good breakfast or snack meal. The canned herrings are served as they are in hors d'oeuvre or as a dish by themselves or with salad. Frozen whole herrings are de-frosted and cooked like fresh herrings.

Hake is sold frozen in steaks and is cooked like fresh fish.

Halibut is sold frozen as fillets or steaks and is cooked as fresh fish.

Kippers are sold frozen, including the cook-in-a-bag kind. They are also available canned. Fresh kippers are sold either whole or filleted. The best ones are oak-smoked and not dyed. To grill, see page 81.

Lemon Sole are available as frozen fillets, defrosted and cooked as fresh.

Lobster sold canned and used to make salads, sandwich fillings and to garnish other fish dishes or to make a sauce to serve with fish.

Mackerel is sold canned or smoked. The smoked is already cooked and is served as it is with horseradish sauce. The canned is used for salads, sandwiches and on toast.

Mussels are sold canned and in jars. They can be served as hors d'oeuvre with lemon and brown bread and butter or use them to make a sauce to serve with other fish or to make a soup.

Oysters are sold canned and used as hors d'oeuvre, or to make sauces or soup.

Pilchards are sold canned and used in the same way as canned herrings or mackerel.

Plaice is sold frozen, as fillets or small whole plaice. They are defrosted and cooked as fresh plaice.

Prawns sold as peeled frozen or as canned. Either can be used in the same way as fresh prawns, as a dish on their own or to make salads, open sandwiches or to serve with other fish as a garnish. Canned curried prawns are sold ready for re-heating and serving with rice.

Salmon is available as frozen, canned or smoked. Frozen steaks are defrosted and then cooked as fresh salmon. Canned salmon is used for salads, sandwiches and for hot savoury dishes, while smoked salmon is used for hors d'oeuvre or sandwiches. Frozen salmon is best cooked 'en Papilotte'—see Herrings en Papilotte.

Sardines are sold canned in oil and are used for hors d'oeuvre, in salads, on toast or open sandwiches.

Scampi are sold frozen or canned and are served in the same way as prawns.

Shrimps are sold canned and used in the same way as prawns. Frozen potted shrimps are de-frosted and served for hors d'oeuvre.

Sprats are sold smoked and used for hors d'oeuvre.

Trout is available either as frozen or smoked. The frozen are de-frosted and cooked like fresh trout and the smoked are served with lemon or horseradish sauce and brown bread and butter either for hors d'oeuvre or as a snack meal. Also available canned when they are used like other canned fish.

Tuna is sold canned and used in the same way as canned salmon.

Whiting fillets are sold frozen and are defrosted before cooking as fresh fish.

FISH FRIED IN BUTTER. The easiest, quickest and most delicious fried fish. Suitable for fresh or frozen fish.

Milk: flour: salt and pepper: wedges of lemon: parsley

Use fillets, steaks or small whole fish. Dip the fish in milk to moisten it and then roll it in a mixture of flour, salt and pepper to coat well. Heat enough butter to cover the bottom of the frying pan and fry the fish until it is golden brown on both sides. Drain and serve with lemon wedges and a parsley garnish.

FRIED FISH A LA MEUNIERE. Proceed as above but add a little more butter to the pan after the fish has been removed and put to keep hot. Heat the butter until it turns nut brown and then pour it quickly over the fish.

GRILLED FISH. Suitable for fresh, frozen or smoked fish.

COOKING TIME: 5–15 mins depending on thickness:
QUANTITIES 1 steak or small fish per person

Small whole fish can either be split down the belly and opened out flat, pressing along the backbone from the outside to make them stay flat; or cut several gashes in each side to help the heat to penetrate.

Brush white fish with oil but oily fish like herrings need no additional oil. Heat the grill and place the fish on the grid or in the bottom of the grill pan. If this is first lined with foil, it cuts down the washing-up afterwards. Grill gently until the fish is brown on one side and the flesh is showing opaque for about half the depth. Turn and grill the other side.

Serve at once with wedges of lemon and a knob of butter and garnished with parsley or watercress. Alternatively, serve a sauce such as Brown Butter Sauce, page 57, or Tartare Sauce, page 62, or use bottled Tartare or other sauce.

BARBECUE BASTING SAUCE FOR GRILLED FISH

QUANTITIES for 4

2 Tbs oil: 1–2 tsp lemon juice: ¼ tsp salt: pinch of pepper

Mix together and spoon or brush over the fish during cooking. For variety add to it any one of the following:

1 tsp French mustard: 1 tsp Worcester sauce: 1 Tbs chopped olives: 1 tsp anchovy sauce: 1–2 Tbs wine: 1 Tbs chopped gherkins: ½ tsp grated horseradish: 1 Tbs ketchup

BAKED FISH WITH WINE

COOKING TIME: 20–30 mins: QUANTITIES for 4
TEMPERATURE: E 375°, G 5

1 small fillet or steak or whole fish per person: vegetables such as dried onion or sliced mushrooms or a little chopped tomato with some onion: salt and pepper

Put a layer of vegetable in the dish with the fish on top. Season with salt and pepper.

White wine or cider: butter or margarine

Add sufficient liquid to moisten the vegetables and put a few knobs of butter or margarine on top. Bake in a moderate oven basting once or twice and cook until the flakes separate easily when tested with a fork. Drain the fish and keep hot.

Roux

Thicken the liquid with a little roux and pour over the fish.

FISH WITH PINEAPPLE

COOKING TIME: 10 mins: QUANTITIES for 4

1 lb fillets white fish, fresh or frozen (½ kg)

Grill or bake the fish and while it is cooking make the sauce as follows:

2 oz roux (60 g): ½ pt milk (1 c or ¼ l)

Heat the milk, add roux and stir until it thickens. Cook for a minute. Alternatively, use one-stage method, page 54.

8 oz chopped canned pineapple (1 c or 250 g): salt and pepper: ⅛ pt double cream (¼ c or ¾ dl)

Add to the sauce and heat without allowing to boil. Pour over the fish.

Chopped parsley or paprika pepper.

Sprinkle with parsley or pepper to garnish. Serve hot.

SMOKED FISH HOTPOT

COOKING TIME: 20 mins: TEMPERATURE E 375°, G 5: QUANTITIES for 4

12 oz smoked fish fillets, fresh or defrosted (375 g): 12 oz tomatoes (375 g)

Slice the tomatoes. Put the fish in an oiled baking dish with the tomatoes on top.

½ tsp pepper: 1 oz butter (2 Tbs or 30 g)

Sprinkle the tomatoes with pepper and dot with butter

2 Tbs water: 4–8 thin rashers bacon

Add the water and cover with the bacon. Bake until the fish flakes easily when tested with a fork. Serve hot with:

Mashed potatoes

SOUSED FISH. Easy to prepare and cooks unattended in a slow oven. Makes a useful cold dish.

COOKING TIME: 1½–2 hrs:

QUANTITIES for 4: TEMPERATURE E 275°, G 2

4 herrings or equivalent amount of other small fish, fresh or frozen also suitable for thick pieces of fillet or steaks

Wash the cleaned fish and pack into a casserole.

1 onion, fresh or dried: 6 cloves: 1 tsp peppercorns: 1 tsp salt: 1 1 tsp sugar: 1 bay leaf

If fresh onion is used, peel and slice it. Add onion and seasonings to the fish.

½ pt vinegar (1 c or ¼ l) or half wine and half water

Add the liquid, cover and cook slowly for at least 1½ hrs. Remove the lid and leave in the dish to become cold. Store in the refrigerator. Serve with some of the liquid as a sauce.

FRIED HERRING ROES. Defrost frozen roes or drain canned ones. Wash and drain fresh roes. Dip them in seasoned flour and fry quickly in a little hot oil or butter until they are lightly browned. Serve on toast with lemon wedges and garnish with parsley.

BAKED HERRINGS EN PAPILLOTE

COOKING TIME: 30 mins: QUANTITIES allow 1 herring per person TEMPERATURE E 375–400°, G 5–6

Remove heads, tails and fins from the cleaned fish. Season the insides with:

Salt and pepper: a little lemon juice

Wrap each fish in a parcel of foil. Put in a baking dish and cook for ½ hr. Remove from the foil and serve with any liquid surrounding it. Serve with:

Mustard sauce: boiled potatoes

BOILED HERRINGS

COOKING TIME: 6 mins: QUANTITIES for 4

4 fresh or defrosted herrings: 1½ pt water (3 c or ¾ l): 2 oz salt (3 Tbs or 60 g)

Remove heads and tails from the cleaned fish. Bring water and salt to the boil, add the fish and boil with the water at a gallop for 6 minutes. Remove the fish, drain and serve hot with a sauce or cold with salad.

Suitable sauces are: *Mustard, tomato, onion or parsley.*

HERRINGS FRIED IN OATMEAL

COOKING TIME: 10 mins: QUANTITIES for 4

4 fresh or defrosted herrings: 1 tsp salt: fat or oil for frying: 4 Tbs fine or coarse oatmeal

Remove heads, tails and fins from the cleaned fish. Leave whole or bone and open out flat. Mix oatmeal and salt and coat the fish with this. Fry in the hot fat or oil until the fish is brown on both sides. Garnish with:

Parsley and lemon

Serve with:

Boiled potatoes

FISH WITH CHUTNEY SAUCE

COOKING TIME: 20 mins: QUANTITIES for 4

*4 fillets or slices of frozen fish: 1 bay leaf: ½ pt water (1 c or ¼ l):
1 tsp salt*

Put in a saucepan or casserole and cook very gently until the fish
separates easily when tested with a fork. Lift out the fish and keep
hot; remove bay leaf.

2 oz white roux (60 g)

Add to the hot liquid and stir until it boils. Boil 5 mins.

3 Tbs chutney: salt and pepper to taste: squeeze of lemon juice

Add to the sauce and re-heat. Pour over the fish and serve hot.

FISH COCKTAIL

QUANTITIES for 4

*Allow about ½ pt prepared shellfish (1 c or ¼ l): 4 lettuce leaves
or other salad vegetables*

Shred the vegetable and put a little in the bottom of individual
glasses. Ordinary large wine glasses are suitable.

Put the fish on top of the salad and pour onto it the following
sauce:

*¼ pt tomato ketchup (½ c or 1½ dl): 1 tsp Worcester sauce:
1 Tbs horseradish sauce: 1 tsp French mustard: ¼ pt canned
cream (½ c or 1½ dl): brandy or liqueur (optional): ½ Tbs
lemon juice*

Combine ingredients and pour over the fish. Garnish the tops with:

Parsley or other green herbs

Serve chilled.

ALTERNATIVE SAUCE FOR THE FISH COCKTAIL

*¼ pt tomato juice (½ c or 1½ dl): ¼ pt yoghurt (½ c or 1½
dl)*

Use these instead of the ketchup and cream in the previous recipe.

BAKED FISH AU GRATIN

COOKING TIME: 20–30 mins: TEMPERATURE E 375°, G 5:
QUANTITIES: allow 1 steak or small fish per person.

4 pieces fresh or frozen fish: fat: brown breadcrumbs: ½–¾ pt
sauce: cheese, tomato, mustard, or a concentrated soup (1½–4 dl)

Oil a shallow fireproof dish and put the washed fish in a single layer in the bottom. Mask with the sauce. Sprinkle the top with browned crumbs, dot with butter or margarine. Bake until the fish flakes easily when tested with a fork. Serve at once.

MARINATED FISH STEAKS

COOKING TIME: 12 mins: QUANTITIES for 4

1 bay leaf: 1 sprig thyme or ½ tsp dried thyme: ¼ pt wine vinegar
(½ c or 1½ dl)

Heat to boiling point and then cool.

4 fish steaks or pieces of thick fillet

Put in a shallow dish and pour the cold marinade over the fish. Leave for ½ hr, turning once. Drain off the marinade, season the fish with salt and pepper, brush with oil and grill for 12 mins, or until the fish is tender.

Lemon wedges: butter

Serve fish with a knob of butter on top and garnished with lemon wedges.

CHAPTER TWELVE

Meat

THE four basic methods of cooking meat, roasting, boiling, frying and grilling, do not require much time for preparation nor much attention during cooking, especially if an automatic oven is used for the first two. Some methods of stewing require the preparation of many ingredients and preliminary frying but there are simple modifications and I have included some of these.

For tips on buying and storing meat see pages 27 and 34–6.

HYGIENE IN MEAT HANDLING

Unless meat is handled in a clean manner it can be a source of food poisoning and the busy cook can easily get into careless ways.

Most important is to see that all meat is thoroughly cooked and that if it is to be served cold it is cooled as quickly as possible and then stored in the refrigerator. It should then not be brought out until it is to be served.

If cooked meat is being re-heated in any way, it must be brought up to boiling temperature to make it safe and preferably kept at this heat for a few minutes—just warming up is very dangerous.

Bought meat pies and cooked meat should be used up on the day of purchase.

CANNED MEAT

Practically every variety of meat is canned as well as many well-known made-up meat dishes such as curries, goulash, Irish stew, meat balls, stewed steak, mince, quenelles, fricassées, beef stroganoff, steak and kidney pudding and pie, braised steak, Lancashire hotpot, Chilli con Carne, meat pie fillings.

Canned meat has to be processed at a high temperature to make it keep safely and this inevitably leads to over-cooking and to a twice-cooked taste when it is re-heated. The most useful of the canned meats are plain things like stewed or braised steak and mince which can be used in a variety of ways as a basis for quick dishes of your own devising. The addition of other ingredients helps to disguise the fact that the meat has come out of a tin. See recipes, pages 101–2.

Canned meat to be served cold is a different matter. Some of it is very good, with varieties to suit all tastes. Read the labels before buying as these tell whether the contents are all meat or whether there are other ingredients such as bread and vegetables.

Varieties of canned cold meats include chopped pork and ham, pork brawn, roast meats, ham and beef roll, corned beef, ham, pork luncheon meat, tongue, frankfurters, sausages, pâté, chopped cured pork, brisket of beef and boned pigs trotters.

MEAT FROM THE FREEZER

Minced meat burgers, lamb or pork chops, and sausages are the main raw meats available from the commercial freezer. Fresh meat you buy from the butcher may be stored in your own freezer. It can be cooked from the frozen state or defrosted. After defrosting, the cooking times are the same as for fresh meat. If it is cooked in the frozen state, it will take at least twice as long as when unfrozen and it is advisable to allow plenty of extra time. If chops and steaks are being cooked, the heat should be more gentle than for unfrozen meat.

Defrosting times: Thick steaks (1 in or 2½ cm), 12–18 hours in the refrigerator or 2–3 hours at room temperature. Small roasts 3–5 hours per lb (½ *kg*) in the refrigerator or 1–2 hours per lb at room temperature. Large roasts 4–7 hours per lb (½ kg) in the refrigerator, 2–3 hours at room temperature.

Some cooked meats are available from the commercial freezer but many of them tend to taste re-heated. Home-made stews, such as curries, goulash and others, provided they do not contain potatoes, can be frozen satisfactorily. After the initial cooking, the meat must be cooled as quickly as possible before freezing. Surrounding the casserole with iced water helps to speed cooling. When it is quite cold, freeze at the coldest setting. Meat may be frozen in the casserole, then removed and wrapped and returned to the casserole for re-heating. Alternatively, line the casserole with foil, freeze and then lift out the foil and stew and wrap. It can be dropped back into the casserole when required.

Sliced cooked meat to be served cold can be stored in the freezer in small polythene boxes. If it is to be kept more than a few weeks the meat must be covered by sauce or stock. Defrost in the refrigerator or at room temperature.

DRIED MEATS

These are the newest of the preserved meats, being accelerated freeze-dried, that it, frozen and then dried. They are chiefly available in packets with ingredients to make a complete meal, e.g. curry and rice. Quality is generally good and the food does not have a re-heated taste. There will undoubtedly be more of this in the future.

THE COLD MEAT PLATTER

This is an interesting way of serving cold meat and salad, seen at its best in many European countries where a large variety of sausages and cold meats are available. The platter is a large serving dish or small tray with many different kinds of sliced cold meats arranged on it, garnished with gherkins or other pickles, tomato, hard-boiled eggs, cucumber, potato salad or Russian salad. Some of the meat can be bought from the delicatessen, though if you keep a variety of small tins of meats, it is possible to make up a platter from store, possibly helped out with some meat from a cold joint or sliced cooked meat from the home freezer. It is obviously not a very practical thing for just two people but is ideal for six or more.

ROASTING

The most trouble-free method of roasting is the low-temperature method because it always gives a tender result with minimum shrinkage of the meat and there is no fat splashed on the oven to make cleaning tedious. It is also a good method to use in the automatic oven. Spit roasting is not so versatile as far as shapes and sizes and cuts are concerned, but it too is an easy method. Wrapping meat in foil is a good method when the oven is wanted for other foods requiring a high temperature, such as pastry and Yorkshire pudding. The foil prevents fat from splashing onto the oven lining which is otherwise unavoidable at high temperatures. It also prevents shrinkage and dryness. Open up the foil for the last ½ hour of cooking to allow the meat to brown.

CUTS TO USE

Beef Sirloin, topside, thick flank, top rib, fore rib, back rib, brisket, a large piece of rump steak.
Lamb Leg, shoulder, loin, best end of neck.
Pork Loin, leg, hand and spring, spare ribs.
Veal Leg, loin, boned and rolled shoulder, breast.

TEMPERATURE

Slow Roasting E 325°, G 3 for beef, lamb or veal: E 375°, G 4 for pork. *Foil Wrapped* E 450°, G 8.

COOKING TIMES (for either method)

Beef Unboned ribs and thin pieces—40 mins per lb (½ kg).
Boned and rolled and thick pieces—45 mins per lb (½ kg).
For underdone meat use approximately ⅔ of these times.
Lamb 45 mins per lb (½ kg).
Pork Spare ribs and loin 35 mins per lb (½ kg). Leg 40 mins per lb (½ kg).
Veal Pieces with bone 30 mins per lb (½ kg). Boned and rolled 40 mins per lb (½ kg).

QUANTITIES With bone allow 8–12 oz per person (250–375 g); no bone allow 4–6 oz per person (120–180 g).

METHOD

Place the meat in a roasting pan or other oven-proof dish. Lean meat like veal should either be covered with rashers of fat bacon or with a loose lid of foil. To obtain crisp crackling with pork, rub the rind with salt or brush with oil and be sure to put the meat in the tin in such a way that the rind is kept above the drippings. Putting the meat on a wire rack is ideal.

At these low temperatures there should be no need to baste the meat.

When the meat is ready, remove it to a hot dish and put to keep warm. Pour off surplus fat from the pan and then add stock or vegetable water to the drippings. Bring to the boil, stirring well to dissolve any bits stuck to the pan. Season and serve either over the meat or in a separate sauce boat. If the roasting pan is not suitable for putting on the burner or hotplate pour the gravy into a small pan and bring to the boil. See also Gravy, page 60.

MEAT IN THE AUTOMATIC OVEN

If you are out all day and want to have a hot meal ready by the time you get home in the evening the answer is to use the automatic oven control. This does, of course, mean that the meat has to be put in the oven early in the morning. It should be very fresh and in good condition, otherwise it may develop a tainted flavour before the cooking begins. Frozen meat can be used but put it in the oven in time to allow complete defrosting otherwise it is difficult to estimate cooking times. See MEAT FROM THE FREEZER.

THE ROTISSERIE OR SPIT ROASTER

Most suitable for poultry, boned and rolled joints and for pieces of meat on skewers; see KEBABS.

Meat does not need basting. If it is very lean, tie a piece of fat over the lean surface and this will act as a baster. Remove the fat towards the end of cooking to allow the meat to brown.

COOKING TIMES Joints 20–30 mins per lb (½ kg). For smaller pieces of meat, times are the same as for grilling under a moderate heat.

BOILING

This is a very simple method of cooking requiring little preparation of ingredients and the minimum of attention. It can be done on top of the stove, in the oven, or in a pressure cooker at 15 lb pressure.

Both fresh and salt meats may be boiled, and it is a good way of cooking the less tender cuts. Cold boiled meat is moist and pleasant to serve with salad, and for sandwiches.

Boiling fresh meat. There are three methods to choose from:

1. Boiling in water with vegetables and seasonings, the stock eventually being used for a sauce to serve with the meat and the remainder for a soup.
2. Wrapping the meat in a parcel of foil with vegetables and flavourings and boiling in water. Any liquid inside the foil is used to make the sauce to serve with the meat.
3. In the pressure cooker with vegetables and flavourings. The amount of cooking liquid is less than with method 1 and the liquid has more flavour. It is used to make a sauce to serve with the meat and any left can be added to a soup.

Prepare the vegetables. For Methods 1 and 2, heat enough water in the pan to come half-way up the sides of the meat. Add ½ Tbs salt. Put meat and vegetables in and reduce heat to simmering. For method 3 allow ½–1 pt water (¼–½ l) and 1 tsp salt. To serve, slice the meat and surround with the vegetables. If the meat is to be served cold, cool it as quickly as possible, not in the cooking liquid, and then store in the refrigerator. Strain the stock, cool and refrigerate until required.

COOKING TIMES AND CUTS USED Methods 1 and 2.

Beef The usual joints are silverside, brisket or topside. For pieces weighing 1 lb (½ kg) or less, allow 1 hr; 2–3 lb (1–1½ kg) allow 2–3 hrs; 4–5 lb (2–2½ kg) allow 3–4 hrs. For larger pieces allow 20 mins per lb (½ kg) plus 20 mins.
Lamb or Mutton Mutton is the traditional one for boiling but lamb may be used too. The usual joints are leg, shoulder or boned and rolled breast. Allow 30 mins per lb (½ kg) plus 30 mins.
Veal Boned and rolled breast is the cut usually boiled and it is frequently stuffed. For one breast of veal allow 1½–2 hrs and if it is to be stuffed, allow 4 oz (120 g) dry weight of stuffing, veal forcemeat being the usual one.

COOKING TIME FOR PRESSURE COOKING: At 15 lb pressure allow ⅓–¼ of the above times.

QUANTITIES

Allow 4–6 oz (125–200) per person without bone: 8–12 oz (250–375 g) with bone.

Vegetables to cook with the meat: onions, carrots, parsnips, turnips, celery.

Flavourings bouquet garni, cloves, peppercorns, salt and pepper.

Accompaniments Serve with the vegetables cooked round the meat. The cooking liquid can be served as a sauce without thickening or use it to make a parsley, caper or tomato sauce. Horseradish sauce is served with boiled beef and onion or caper sauce with boiled mutton or lamb.

Boiling Salt Meat

Method 1 above is the best if the meat is really salt. Lightly salted meat can be cooked by methods 2 and 3. Before cooking, salt meat should be soaked over-night in cold water to cover, or at least soak for 3–4 hrs. Otherwise the method is the same as for fresh meat, except that the meat goes into unsalted cold water instead of boiling water.

Salt Meats Used for Boiling Bacon joints, ham, salt pork, salt beef.

KEBOB: KABOB: KEBAB: SHASHLIK. These consist of small pieces of meat grilled on skewers with vegetables. The meat is usually served with a rice dish but sometimes also with potatoes and salad.

Suitable meats are small pieces of lamb, frying steak, pork, liver, kidneys, bacon, sausages, pieces of chicken. The vegetables used may be mushrooms, tomatoes, sweet peppers, onions, aubergine, cucumber and fruits such as apple, raw or canned peaches, canned apricots, prunes, bananas, pineapple chunks, orange segments, olives.

Cut the meat into 1–1½ in (3 cm) cubes. Be sure all vegetables and fruits are firm. Cut quick cooking ones in large pieces and slower cooking ones in small pieces. Thread them onto special long skewers alternating meat with the other ingredients of choice. Moisten the food by brushing with oil or a basting sauce, see page 56. Grill quickly turning often; time about 15 mins.

BAKED BACON. This is very easy to prepare. Serve some hot with vegetables and use the rest as cold meat. Choose one of the mild cured pieces especially sold for cooking in a piece. If salty bacon is used it must be soaked and parboiled before cooking as follows.

COOKING TIME: 30 mins per lb (½ kg):
QUANTITIES: Allow 4 oz per portion (125 g):
TEMPERATURE E 325°, G 5

Put the bacon in a roasting pan or oven-proof dish and cook plain or with a basting sauce; see below.

If preferred, the bacon may be wrapped in foil but in this case allow 45 mins per lb (½ kg). Open the foil for the last half-hour of cooking and increase the heat to E 375°, G 5 to allow the meat to brown. Add the basting sauce at this stage.

BASTING SAUCES FOR BAKED BACON

1. Brush the meat with melted red currant jelly and put a little red wine in the pan.
2. Put a tablespoon of black treacle on top of the meat and a little cider round it.
3. Put a tablespoon of black treacle on top and pour stout round it.
4. Put a tablespoon of honey on top and pour orange juice round it.
5. Mix ½ oz dry mustard (1½ Tbs or 15 g), ½ oz sugar (1 Tbs or 15 g) and ⅛ pt orange juice (¼ c or ¾ dl) and pour over the meat.

GRILLED GAMMON

COOKING TIME: 10–20 mins:
QUANTITIES one rasher per person or half a very thick one

The rashers are usually cut ¼–½ in (½–1 cm) thick. If they seem salty, soak them in warm water for ½–1 hr. Drain and dry on paper towels. Remove the rind with scissors and snip the fat at intervals of about 1 in to help keep the rasher flat during cooking. Preheat the grill and cook the gammon until the fat looks clear, turning frequently during cooking. Cooking with a moderate heat gives best results. Garnishes to grill with the gammon can be:

Tomatoes: mushrooms: apple rings: canned peach halves: pineapple slices

Or serve with spinach to make the traditional English dish of 'Gammon and Spinach'.

GRILLED BEEF STEAK

COOKING TIME: 10–15 mins:
QUANTITIES allow 6–8 oz per portion (200–250 g)

The meat should be not less than 1 in (2½ cm) thick, otherwise it tends to become dry. Frying is a better method for thin slices.

Cuts used are fillet, rump, sirloin, porterhouse; small pieces of steak about 2 in (5 cm) square are called tournedos, mignon or noisettes. Also see KEBABS.

Brush the steak with oil and preheat the grill. Cook the steak under a fierce heat for 1 min each side, then reduce the heat slightly or move the meat further away from the grill and continue cooking, turning every 2 mins. Put on a hot dish with the chosen garnish, and pour any juices in the pan over it. Season with salt and pepper.
Garnishes:

Watercress: grilled tomatoes: grilled mushrooms: chip potatoes

FRIED STEAK AND ONIONS

COOKING TIME: 10–15 mins for the onion and 5–15 mins for the steak, depending on its thickness and whether you like it well done or rare; QUANTITIES for 4

1–2 lb rump steak (½–1 kg): 1½ lb onions (750 g): salt and pepper: a little butter

Have the meat cut in 4 portions. Trim off excess fat and cut it in small pieces. Peel the onions and put them in a slicer to make ⅛ in (3 mm) slices. Season the meat. Put the chopped fat in a heavy frying pan and heat until the fat runs. Remove fat and add the onions. Reduce the heat and cook gently, stirring frequently until the onions are tender and lightly browned. Remove and keep hot.

Add a small nut of butter to the pan and turn up the heat. When the butter begins to brown add the steaks. Brown each side quickly and continue to cook over a good heat until they are done as required. Turn every minute or two. Serve on a hot dish with the onions. Add a little water or stock to the pan and stir and simmer until the sediment in the pan is dissolved. Pour this over the steak.

FRIED FILLET OF BEEF WITH MUSHROOM SAUCE

COOKING TIME: 20 mins: QUANTITIES for 4

1 oz butter (2 Tbs or 30 g): 4 pieces fillet steak cut 1 in (2½ cm) thick

Heat the butter in a deep frying pan or shallow stew pan. Put in the steaks and brown them very quickly, 2 mins each side. Remove them from the pan.

½ oz flour (1½ Tbs or 15 g): ½ pt stock (1 c or ¼ dl) or red wine: salt and pepper

Add flour to the fat in the pan and mix well, cooking for a few minutes. Add the liquid and stir until it boils. Season well.

8 oz mushrooms

Wash and slice the mushrooms. Add them to the sauce and boil gently for 10 mins, adding stock or water as necessary. Add the steaks and simmer for 5 mins.

Watercress

Wash and drain and use to garnish the steaks.

TOPSIDE COOKED IN WINE

COOKING TIME: 4 hrs: TEMPERATURE E 250°, G ½: QUANTITIES for 6–8

2½–3 lb piece of topside of beef (1¼–1½ kg)

If this has been sold with a piece of fat tied round, remove before cooking.

Salt and pepper

Season meat and rub in well.

1 Tbs dry mustard: 1 Tbs flour: milk to mix

D

Mix the mustard and flour to a paste with milk and spread it over the meat. Put meat in a casserole just large enough to hold it.

2 *onions, sliced:* 1/4 *pt red wine* (1/2 *c or* 1 1/2 *dl*): 2 *Tbs wine vinegar*

Add to the pan. Cover and cook very slowly.

4–8 *mushrooms* 125–250 *g*): *oil*

Brush mushrooms with oil and grill until just tender.

Slice meat and put on a serving dish with some of the cooking liquor.

Garnish with the mushrooms.

The rest of the meat will be excellent to serve cold. Use any remaining liquor in a soup.

BEEF STEAK WITH LEMON

COOKING TIME: 45 mins: QUANTITIES for 4

1 1/2 *lb rump steak* (750 *g*)

Trim off surplus fat and cut it in small pieces. Heat it in a shallow stewpan until the fat begins to run. Meanwhile, cut the steak in 4 portions. Remove bits of fat from the pan and add the steak.

8 *thin slices of lemon*

When the steak is brown on one side, turn and add the pieces of lemon, cover the pan and stew very slowly for 10–15 mins.

1/8 *pt marsala or port wine* (1/4 *c or* 3/4 *dl*): 1/8 *pt water* (1/4 *c or* 1 *dl*): 1 *meat cube: salt and pepper*

Add to the meat and simmer for a few minutes without the lid to allow some of the liquid to evaporate.

1 *Tbs lemon juice*

Add to the pan. Serve the steak with the sauce poured over it. If liked, the sauce may be thickened with a little potato flour, blended with cold water.

BEEF GOULASH—Pressure cooked—(suitable for freezing)

COOKING TIME: 35 mins at 15 lb pressure: QUANTITIES for 3–4

1 *lb lean stewing steak* (½ *kg*): 1 *oz fat or oil* (2 *Tbs or 30 g*)

Trim off surplus fat and cut the meat in small pieces (½–1 inch cubes or 1–2 cm). Heat fat or oil and fry the meat in it until brown.

2 *onions*

Peel and slice and add to the meat. Continue cooking until the onion begins to brown.

2 *tsp paprika pepper*

Add to the meat and mix well

½ *pt water* (1 *c or* ¼ *l*): 1 *meat cube*: ½ *tsp salt*: *pinch of carra-way seeds* 2 *Tbs tomato paste*

Add to the meat and pressure cook for about 30 mins. Allow the pressure to reduce and serve with:

Boiled cabbage and boiled potatoes

BRAZILIAN BEEF (suitable for freezing). This requires little preparation but long, slow cooking.

COOKING TIME 3 hrs: QUANTITIES for 4
TEMPERATURE E 275–300°, G 1–2

1 ½ *lb stewing beef* (750 g): *wine vinegar*

Ask the butcher to cut the meat in 8 pieces. Dip them in a little vinegar and put in a casserole. Cook very slowly without any liquid until tender.

1 *tsp Worcester or Soy sauce*: 1 *Tbs red wine or port*: *salt to taste*: *brown roux to thicken, or use potato starch or cornflour*

Add these to the stock which has come from the meat and heat until it thickens. If brown roux is not used for thickening, it may be necessary to add a little browning to the sauce.

CURRIED BEEF (to make for storage in the freezer)

COOKING TIME: 2½–3 hrs: QUANTITIES for 4

1 ½ *lb stewing beef* (750 g): 1 ½ *oz flour* (4½ *Tbs or 45 g*): 2 *tsp salt*

Ask the butcher to cut the meat in small pieces. Mix flour and salt in a paper bag and shake the meat in this to coat it.

2 medium sized onions: ½ clove garlic: 2 apples: 1 tomato

Peel and chop the onion, apples and garlic. Chop the tomato.

2 oz dripping or oil (4 Tbs or 60 g): 2 Tbs curry powder

Heat the dripping in a pan or fireproof casserole, fry the meat and then the vegetables. Add curry powder and fry a few minutes longer.

½ pt stock made with meat cube and water (1 c or ¼ l): 1 tsp brown sugar: 1 Tbs desiccated coconut (more if liked): rind and juice of ½ lemon: 2 Tbs raisins or sultanas

Stir in the stock and add the other ingredients. Cover and cook slowly, the longer the better. If cooked in the oven use E 300°, G ½. It can be cooked in the pressure cooker but the flavour is not so rich.

STEAK AND KIDNEY PIE. This is easy to assemble and cook if the meat is bought ready cut up and the pastry ready-made or use quick method see page 196.

COOKING TIME: 2 hrs: QUANTITIES for 6–8
TEMPERATURE: E 450°, G 8 for 10–15 mins. Then E 350°, G ½ for the remainder of the time.

2½ lb steak and kidney cut in pieces (1¼ kg): 1 Tbs flour: 1 tsp salt: ½ tsp pepper: hot water

Mix flour and seasonings in a paper bag. Put in the meat and shake to coat it well. Pack the meat into a 2 pint size (1 l) pie-dish piling it up in the centre. Add hot water to three-quarters fill the dish.

12 oz short crust, puff or flaky pastry (375 g)

Roll the pastry to ¼–½ in (1 cm) thick and about 2 in (5 cm) larger than the top of the pie-dish. Cut a strip of pastry to go round the rim of the dish and fasten it in position with water to moisten. Lift the large piece of pastry on top of the pie, easing it into position. Press down round the rim and trim off surplus pastry.

Crimp the edges and cut a hole in the centre to let out steam.

Beaten egg or milk

Brush the top of the pie with this and bake at the higher temperature to brown the crust and then reduce the heat, covering the pastry with foil if it gets too brown.

USING CANNED STEWED STEAK. This is a very useful variety of canned meat to keep in the store cupboard. It is the most satisfactory of the canned meats for making a hot dish. Serve it as a casserole, a sauce for spaghetti or other pasta, with boiled rice, in a nest of mashed potato or make it into a pie with one of the quick pastries.

Any of the following can be added to vary the flavour:

  Worcester or Soy sauce, mushroom ketchup or other ketchup or chutney
  Fried onions
  Fried, or canned sliced mushrooms
  Stoned black olives and a little red wine
  Canned tomatoes or some tomato paste
  Chopped gherkins or other pickles
  Plenty of chopped fresh herbs
  Some red wine, beer or stout
  Canned curry sauce
  Paprika pepper and noodles to serve with it
  Add some canned peas, carrots or mixed canned vegetables
  Some chopped fried bacon

USING A CAN OF MINCE

QUANTITIES for 4

15 oz can of minced beef (450 g): 2 canned red sweet peppers, chopped: 1 oz mushrooms, or a few stalks, chopped (30 g): 1 Tbs chutney: salt and pepper

Heat these together for 5–10 mins.

1½ lb mashed potato (750 g): spinach or other vegetable

If packet potato powder is used, add butter and chopped chives or parsley.

Make a ring of the potatoes and pour the mince into the centre. Serve with a green vegetable.

Method 2 Use it as a sauce to serve with spaghetti, see page 181, or with marcaroni or noodles.

Method 3 QUICK SHEPHERD'S PIE

15 oz can of minced beef (450 g): Worcester sauce, ketchup or chutney to taste: 1 ½ lb mashed potatoes (750 g)

Heat the mince to boiling and season to taste. Put in a hot pie-dish and cover with a layer of freshly prepared mashed potatoes, using packet variety for speed. Brush the top with oil and brown under the grill or in the top of a hot oven.

GRILLED LAMB STEAKS WITH RED CURRANT JELLY

COOKING TIME: 25 mins: QUANTITIES for 4

1 ½–2 lb lamb steaks (¾–1 kg) cut 1 in (3 cm) thick from the leg

Grill the steaks under a moderate heat or on the lowest runner, allowing about 12 mins each side.

4 Tbs red currant jelly

Melt the jelly in a small pan and brush the steaks with it during the last few minutes of cooking. Season the steaks with

Salt and pepper

Serve at once, with more jelly if liked.

GRILLED LAMB CHOPS

COOKING TIME: 10–20 mins: QUANTITIES allow 1 chop per person

Use loin chops and trim off surplus fat. Brush chops with oil and pre-heat the grill. Turn the chops frequently during grilling so that browning and cooking finish together. Serve at once with the chosen garnish.

Garnishes:

A small pat of butter on each chop: mushroom or onion sauce: fried or mashed potatoes: a slice of pineapple or orange put on the chop when it is half cooked, brush fruit with oil and continue cooking

PAPRIKA LAMB

COOKING TIME: about 20 mins: QUANTITIES for 4

2 onions, sliced finely: 2 oz butter (4 Tbs or 60 g)

Heat the butter and brown the onions in it.

½ tsp paprika pepper

Add to the onions and cook a little longer.

*1 lb boned shoulder lamb (½ kg) cut in 1 in cubes (3 cm): 1 Tbs
flour: 1 tsp salt*

Sprinkle the meat with the flour and salt and add it to the onions.
Cover with foil and cook gently until the meat is tender.

A little water, stock, sherry or marsala

Add to the pan to make a very little gravy. Serve as soon as ready.
Serve with:

Sauté or boiled potatoes.

PRESSED LAMB SHOULDER (to serve cold)

COOKING TIME: 2 hrs: QUANTITIES for 6–8: TEMPERATURE E 325°, G 3

1 shoulder lamb

Trim off all surplus fat.

1 clove garlic

Peel and slice and put in the bottom of a casserole or stew pan.
Add the meat.

*½ pt dry white wine (1 c or ¼ l): 2 tsp dried thyme or a sprig of
fresh: ½ tsp dried rosemary or a small sprig of fresh: ½ tsp
dried savory or a sprig of fresh: 1 tsp salt: 1 small bay leaf*

Add to the pan, cover and cook slowly until the bone can easily be
removed from the meat. Place the boned meat in a dish just large
enough to take it. Put a plate and weight on top and leave in a cold
place to cool as quickly as possible. Remove the weight, cover with
foil and store in the refrigerator. To serve, turn out of the dish and
slice thinly. Use the liquid for soup or stock.

IRISH STEW

COOKING TIME: 1½–2 hrs: QUANTITIES for 4

2 lb neck or breast of lamb or mutton (1 kg): 2 lb potatoes (1 kg): 2 large onions

Ask the butcher to cut the meat in pieces. Trim surplus fat from it. Peel the onions and chop or put through a slicer. Peel the potatoes and cut them into thick slices or rough pieces.

1 Tbs salt: ½ tsp pepper

Place a layer of meat in the bottom of a casserole or saucepan, add a layer of potatoes and then of onions and finally seasoning. Repeat the layers. Add cold water to come three-quarters of the way up the meat. Cover and simmer until tender.

This may be done on top of the stove or in the oven at E 300°–325°, G 2–3, but in the latter case, either first bring the stew to the boil on top, or else allow at least an extra 20 minutes for the stew to heat up in the oven.

Plenty of chopped parsley

Serve the stew with parsley sprinkled over. This makes a complete dish and is not usually served with extra vegetables but please yourself about this.

GRILLED KIDNEYS

COOKING TIME: 5–10 mins: QUANTITIES allow 1–2 per person

They may be left whole and with some of the layer of suet still on. Grill gently first one side and then the other until the fat has melted and beads of blood begin to appear on the outside of the kidney. Alternatively, remove the suet, skin the kidneys and remove the hard core with scissors. Either grill them whole, or cut almost through and open out flat like a book. Brush with oil and grill as before.

GRILLED LIVER

COOKING TIME: 5–10 mins: QUANTITIES allow 4 oz per person (125 g)

*Calf's, lamb's, sheep's, or pig's liver cut in ½ in slices:
oil or French dressing*

Brush the liver with oil or dressing and put the slices in the bottom
of the grill pan. Cook until brown each side. Small beads of
blood oozing onto the surface indicate that it is done. Do
not cook beyond this stage or it will become hard and tough.

GRILLED LIVER AND BACON

COOKING TIME: 10 mins: QUANTITIES allow 4 oz liver (125 g) and
1 rasher bacon per person

Put the sliced liver in the bottom of the grill pan and the slices
of bacon over the top. Grill until the bacon is cooked, remove it
and keep hot and continue grilling the liver.

Tomatoes and mushrooms may be grilled with the liver.

FRIED LIVER

COOKING TIME: 5–10 mins:
QUANTITIES allow 4 oz per person (125 g)

Calf's, lamb's, sheep's or pig's liver cut in ½ in (1 cm) slices

Toss the liver in seasoned flour to coat it well.

Heat a mixture of butter and olive oil in a frying pan using just
enough to coat the bottom of the pan. Fry the liver until it is brown
on both sides, turning once during cooking. When the liver is
cooked through, small beads of blood will show on the surface. If
cooked beyond this point it will become hard and tough.

Remove and keep hot.

Swill out the pan with a little stock, boiling, while stirring with a
wooden spoon to dissolve all the bits of sediment. Pour this over
the liver and serve.

FRIED LIVER AND BACON

Cook 1–2 rashers of bacon per person, in the frying pan. Remove
and keep hot. Use this fat plus more if needed to cook the liver as
described above.

LIVER WITH RED WINE

COOKING TIME: 10 mins: QUANTITIES FOR 4

1 lb lamb's or calf's liver (½ kg) cut in ¾ in (2 cm) slices: salt and pepper: 1 oz flour (3 Tbs or 30 g)

Sprinkle the liver with salt and pepper and roll the pieces in flour to coat well.

4 Tbs oil: 1 onion, sliced

Heat the oil and fry the onion until it is tender, about 3 mins. Remove onion and keep hot. Fry liver quickly, 2–3 mins, each side. Return onions.

¼ pt red wine (½ c or 1 ½ dl)

Add to the liver and cook at high heat for 1 min. Serve at once.

FRIED PORK CHOPS

COOKING TIME: 15–20 mins depending on the thickness: QUANTITIES allow one chop per portion

Spare rib or loin chops

Trim off surplus fat.

Lard or oil: a little stock or wine

Heat just enough to cover the bottom of the frying pan.
When it is hot add the chops and brown them quickly on each side. Then reduce the heat to continue the cooking. If the pan has a lid, cover the chops at this stage to help keep them moist.

When the chops are cooked, remove them to a hot dish pour off surplus fat and swill the pan with a little stock or wine. Heat this and pour it over the chops.

Fried tomatoes or mushrooms: redcurrant jelly: fried apple rings or apple sauce
Serve any of these as garnishes for the chops.

VARIATION Sprinkle instant dried onion over the chops during cooking.

FRIED VEAL CHOPS. Cook in the same way as pork chops using half butter and half lard or olive oil. Lemon juice may be used instead of stock or wine for swilling out the pan.
Garnish with parsley and a little finely chopped onion.

FRIED VEAL ESCALOPES. These are thin slices of veal weighing about 3–4 oz each (100–125 g). Fry in the same way as above but they will take only 3–4 mins.

BEANS AND FRANKFURTERS

COOKING TIME: 35 mins: QUANTITIES for 2–4
TEMPERATURE E 375°, G 5 or cook on the hotplate

8 oz frankfurters (250 g)

Cut in half lengthwise and put in a shallow baking dish, or deep frying pan.

8 oz canned baked beans (250 g)

Add to the sausages.

1 Tbs flour: 1 tsp mustard: ⅛ pt water (¼ c or ¾ dl):
⅛ pt tomato ketchup (¼ c or ¾ dl: 2 Tbs vinegar: 2 tsp sugar

In a small saucepan mix flour and mustard to a smooth paste with the water. Add the other ingredients and heat and stir until it thickens. Pour it over the sausages and beans and cook gently for 30 mins, either on top or in the oven.
Serve with:

Green salad

CHAPTER THIRTEEN

Poultry

ALL young birds cook quickly, either by roasting, frying or grilling, while older and tougher ones can be left to cook slowly, without attention, in pot or casserole. With appropriate accompaniments they all make delicious meals, some in the luxury class.

For tips on buying and storing poultry see pages 30 and 35.

Chicken pieces can be used for frying, grilling, casseroles and baked dishes, see recipes

Ready to serve dishes of poultry are available in many forms. These include:

Canned diced chicken in sauce
Chicken curry
Canned whole roast pheasant
Canned whole roast partridge
Turkey supreme, chasseur and with corn
Canned chicken casserole
Ham and chicken
Breast of chicken, canned and frozen
Chicken and rice
Frozen chicken pie

BAKED CHICKEN JOINTS

COOKING TIME: 1 hr: QUANTITIES for 4
TEMPERATURE E 350°, G 4

4 portions young chicken

Wash and dry and put in a single layer in a shallow baking dish.

½ tsp chopped fresh or dried rosemary: ½ tsp pepper: 1 tsp salt. 1 Tbs instant dried onion: ¼ tsp ground ginger: ¼ tsp paprika pepper

Sprinkle these over the chicken.

¼ pt white wine (½ c or 1½ dl)

Pour round the chicken and bake uncovered until the chicken is tender.

BOILED CHICKEN OR FOWL. This method is used for old birds or 'boilers' which are too tough for roasting. Long, slow cooking with liquid is needed to make them tender.

COOKING TIME 1½–2 hrs or longer depending on size and age. ½–¾ hr pressure cooking at 15 lb pressure (½ pt water or ¼ l): QUANTITIES allow 8 oz (250 g) per portion

1 boiling fowl: a piece of lemon

Rub the cleaned and trussed fowl with a piece of cut lemon to help keep the flesh white. Put the fowl in a pan just large enough to hold it comfortably.

1 onion: 1 carrot: a bouquet garni

Peel the vegetables and cut them in pieces. Add vegetables and bouquet garni to the fowl with enough water to cover it.

Bring to the boil, reduce the heat to a simmer and cook until the thigh of the bird feels tender when pierced with a fork.

Serve it with its breast masked with a sauce or cut it in portions and serve on a platter, masking the pieces with sauce. Hand more sauce separately.

SUITABLE SAUCES

Béchamel sauce using some of the cooking stock: parsley sauce using some of the cooking stock

OTHER ACCOMPANIMENTS

Mushrooms and cooked vegetables to garnish: boiled rice, macaroni, noodles or potatoes

CHICKEN FRICASSÉE (using cooked chicken)

COOKING TIME: 15–20 mins: QUANTITIES for 4

12 oz cooked chicken weighed without bone (375 g), or enough for 4 portions

Remove any skin and cut the chicken in small pieces.

½ pt chicken stock using a cube and water (1 c or ¼ l): 1½ oz ready made roux (45 g): pinch of grated nutmeg: salt and pepper

Put the cube in a pan and add the water. Heat until the cube dissolves and then add the roux, stirring and heating until the sauce thickens. Season to taste. Add the chicken and allow to boil for a few minutes.

2 egg yolks: 1 Tbs chopped parsley: juice of ½ lemon

Blend yolks with lemon juice. Remove pan from the heat and stir in the egg mixture. Do not boil again. Add the parsley.

4 grilled or fried bacon rolls (optional)

Serve the chicken with the bacon to garnish; serve the fricassée with potatoes, rice or pasta and a second vegetable or salad.

FRIED CHICKEN (shallow frying)

COOKING TIME: 20–25 mins: QUANTITIES for 4

4 portions frying chicken: 1 oz flour (3 Tbs or 30 g): 2 tsp salt: ¼ tsp pepper

Mix flour and seasonings and put in a paper bag. Shake the pieces of chicken in this way until they are well coated.

Oil or cooking fat

Use a frying pan large enough to let the pieces of chicken lie flat. Heat enough oil or fat in it to come to the depth of about ¼ in. Fry the chicken, turning it until it is brown all over. Then reduce the heat and continue the cooking for another 15–20 mins. Drain well on absorbent paper.

Raw quartered tomatoes: watercress or lettuce

Serve these as a garnish for the chicken.

GRILLED CHICKEN. Pieces of broiler chicken or poussin are used. Half a small chicken makes one portion though quarters of larger ones may be used. Season the pieces with *salt and pepper* and brush with *oil or a barbecue sauce*, see page 56. Grill under a medium heat for about 20 mins, turning frequently and basting with more *oil or sauce*. Serve with *a green salad or with vegetables*.

CHICKEN WITH MARSALA

COOKING TIME: about 40 mins: QUANTITIES for 4–6

A 4 lb chicken cut in pieces (2 kg) or buy enough ready-cut chicken pieces: salt and pepper

Season the chicken with salt and pepper.

2 oz butter (4 Tbs or 60 g)

Heat in a shallow pan and fry the chicken until brown on both sides.

1 onion, sliced

Add to the pan and cook for about 2 minutes. Reduce the heat and add:

⅛ pt water (¼ c or ¾ dl)

Cover the pan and simmer for about 20 minutes or until the chicken is tender.

¼ pt marsala or dark sherry (½ c or 1½ dl)

Add and simmer for 10 minutes more, adding extra water if necessary. Serve with the liquid as a sauce.

CHICKEN PATTIES OR VOL-AU-VENT. Use half the chicken Fricassée recipe page 110, adding some *canned button mushrooms* if liked, or some *chopped, cooked ham*. Use to fill hot ready-made patties or vol-au-vent or make your own from ready-made pastry; see page 198.

CHICKEN IN A POT

COOKING TIME: about 1 hr: QUANTITIES for 4 or 5
TEMPERATURE E 350°, G3

2½–3 lb roasting chicken (1¼–1½ kg): giblets

Wash chicken and giblets. Put giblets in the bottom of a casserole large enough to hold the chicken. Place chicken on top of giblets.

¼ pt water (½ c or 1½ dl): salt and pepper: 2 Tbs white wine

Add the liquid and salt and pepper to taste. Cover the casserole and cook gently until the chicken is tender. Serve with the liquor as gravy. This is a very good way of cooking a chicken to serve cold and is convenient to put in the oven when doing a batch of cooking for meals ahead.

POT ROASTED CHICKEN

COOKING TIME: 1–1¼ hrs: QUANTITIES for 4
TEMPERATURE E 325°, G 3

A 2½–3 lb roasting chicken (1¼–1½ kg): 2 oz butter (4 Tbs or 60 g): 1 tsp salt: ¼ tsp pepper

The chicken should be cleaned and trussed. Use a large casserole or saucepan. Heat the butter in it and fry the chicken until it is brown all over. Sprinkle with salt and pepper, cover and cook in the oven until tender. Have the chicken lying on its side and turn it once or twice during cooking. Carve the chicken, arrange on a serving dish, pour the juices over and garnish with:

Watercress

VARIATION A few sliced mushrooms added after the chicken has been browned.

ROAST CHICKEN. Nowadays these are practically always sold ready plucked, drawn and trussed. Frozen chickens should be left in the wrapper until they are completely thawed which will take about 7–8 hours. Cook chicken within 24 hrs of defrosting. Some shops sell them partly or completely defrosted and ready for cooking right away.

COOKING TIME: Check the weight of the bird and calculate time on the prepared weight. For birds up to 3½ lb (1¾ kg) allow 20 mins per lb (½ kg) plus 20 mins. TEMPERATURE E 375°, G 5. For larger birds allow 1½–2 hrs: TEMPERATURE E 325–350°, G 3. QUANTITIES Allow 8 oz (½ kg) per portion.

Making stuffing is a time-consuming job so use a packet one or omit stuffing and instead put a knob of butter inside the bird or a small onion or a sprig of rosemary. After stuffing, re-tie the legs over the vent.

Brush the bird with oil and put it on a trivet in the roasting pan. Put either a piece of fat bacon or a loose piece of foil over the breast, but remove for the last 20 mins of cooking to allow the breast to brown. The giblets can be cooked in a separate pan with water to make stock or put them under the bird instead of a trivet and then make the gravy in the pan when the bird is cooked.

ACCOMPANIMENTS Small rolls of streaky bacon may be cooked round the bird and also some chipolata sausages. Bread sauce to serve with it is available in packets.

SPIT ROASTING
    Chicken 45–60 mins
    Duckling 15–20 mins per lb (½ kg)
    Small stuffed turkey 20 mins per lb (½ kg)
    Pheasant 15–20 mins per lb (½ kg)
    Other small birds allow ½–¾ hr depending on size

ROAST DUCK OR DUCKLING. Frozen ducks are suitable for roasting. They are sold either defrosted ready for cooking or completely frozen. Allow to defrost completely before cooking (about 7–8 hours) and then use within 24 hrs.

A fresh duck should have the feet and head on so that the purchaser can see its age. A young duck suitable for roasting will have bright yellow feet and bill.

QUANTITIES: A small duck of 3–3½ lb (1½–1¾ kg) will only provide 4–5 portions. For larger ones allow 8 oz (¼ kg) trussed weight per person.
COOKING TIME: Small duck 1¾–1½ hrs. Larger duck 25–30 mins per lb (½ kg): TEMPERATURE: E 325°, G 2

For stuffing use either a packet sage and onion stuffing or an onion and a sprig of sage. Alternatively stuff with half a peeled orange. After cooking cut the orange into segments to serve with the duck, and add the juice and grated rind of the other half to the gravy. Rub a little salt into the skin and place the duck in a baking pan without fat. When it is cooked, lift it out and pour off most of the fat.

Make gravy in the pan using stock from the giblets which can be cooked in water to cover, in a casserole in the oven while the bird is roasting. Orange juice and/or wine can be added to the gravy.

OTHER ACCOMPANIMENTS Roast potatoes and green peas are traditional, with or without apple sauce. Instead of apple sauce, serve orange salad or a tart jelly like red currant or cranberry.

ROAST WILD DUCK. Stuff with sliced apples (frozen ones can be used) and roast as for domestic duck. Serve with bread sauce and gravy. Alternatively, roast unstuffed and serve with orange salad, watercress and gravy, with either roast potatoes or game chips.

ROAST GOOSE. These can vary in size from as little as 6 lb (3 kg) up to 20–24 lb (10–12 kg).

QUANTITIES: Allow about 12 oz trussed weight per person (375 g): COOKING TIME: 6 lb bird (3 kg) 1 hr 40 mins. 12 lb bird (6 kg) 2 hrs 20 mins. 18 lb bird (9 kg) 3 hrs 10 mins. 24 lb bird (12 kg) 4 hrs: TEMPERATURE: E 325°, G 3

For stuffing use packet sage and onion stuffing or stuff with a mixture of chopped prunes and dried apple rings. First soak the prunes in hot water for 5 mins and then remove the stones.

Put the goose in a pan with a piece of foil resting lightly on top, removing it for the last ½ hr of cooking.

ACCOMPANIMENTS: Brown gravy. Apple, gooseberry or bread sauce. Apple and bread sauces are sold ready prepared. Gooseberry sauce can be quickly made by stewing frozen berries with a very little sugar.

ROAST GROUSE

QUANTITIES: An average 1¼ lb (625 g) bird is sufficient for 3 portions: COOKING TIME: 40–50 mins: TEMPERATURE E 325°, G 3

Stuff with a piece of butter and a squeeze of lemon juice and roast in pan.

ACCOMPANIMENTS Fried or grilled bacon rolls, game chips, or crisps, water cress. Gravy made from the pan drippings and giblet stock.

ROAST PARTRIDGE

QUANTITIES: Allow one bird between 2 people:
COOKING TIME: 30 mins: TEMPERATURE E 450°, G 8

Cover the breast with a piece of fat bacon or pork tied on securely. Remove this for the last 5 mins to allow the breast to brown.

Serve with bread sauce.

ROAST PHEASANT

One bird will serve 2–4 people, a brace is usually enough for 5–6 portions: COOKING TIME: 1–1½ hrs:
TEMPERATURE E 325°, G 3

They may be roasted stuffed or unstuffed. Veal forcemeat stuffing is suitable.

Cover the breast with a piece of fat pork or mild bacon removing it for the last 10 mins to allow browning. Cook the giblets round the bird and make gravy in the pan. Serve with bread sauce and water-cress garnish.

ROAST TURKEY. A small turkey weighs 6–8 lb (3–4 kg) and a large one can be 20–25 lb (10–12½ kg) or more. When buying a large one make sure it is not too big for the oven. They are usually sold plucked and drawn. Frozen turkey must be completely defrosted before cooking. Thaw for 4–5 hrs per lb (½ kg) in the refrigerator or 1 hr per lb (½ kg) at room temperature.

QUANTITIES: Allow about 12 oz (375 g) trussed weight per person: COOKING TIME: Trussed weight 6–8 lb (3–4 kg) 3¼–3¾ hrs. 8–10 lb (4–5 kg) 3¾–4¼ hrs. 10–14 lb (5–7 kg) 4¼–4¾ hrs. 14–18 lb (7–9 kg) 4¾–5¼ hrs. 18–20 lb (9–10 kg) 5¼–6¼ hrs. 20–24 lb (10–12 kg) 6¼–7 hrs: TEMPERATURE: E 325°, G 3

Chestnut stuffing is the traditional one and is easy to make with canned chestnut purée and dried breadcrumbs or cornflake crumbs. For a 12–14 lb (6–7 kg) turkey allow:

1 lb chestnut purée (½ kg): 6 oz breadcrumbs (2 c or 200 g): 1 lb pork sausage meat (½ kg): 4 oz melted butter or dripping (125 g): 1 Tbs chopped parsley: 3 tsp salt: ½ tsp pepper: stock or red wine to moisten

Mix all together thoroughly.

Stuff the bird first from the crop end to make it a good plump shape. Cover the opening with the flap of skin and secure with a small skewer. Spoon the remaining stuffing into the body and fasten up with a small skewer tying the crossed legs over the vent.

Place the bird in the roasting pan with a piece of foil resting lightly on top (do not wrap). When the bird has cooked for about two-thirds of the time, cut the string holding the legs together to allow the heat to penetrate to the inside part of the thigh. If necessary for browning, remove the foil for the last ½ hr.

Make gravy in the pan after pouring off surplus fat. Use stock made from the giblets.

ACCOMPANIMENTS Small sausages and bacon rolls can be cooked in a separate pan. In addition to the gravy serve either cranberry sauce (available canned) or bread sauce (packet).

CHICKEN WITH ROSEMARY

COOKING TIME 35–40 mins: QUANTITIES for 4

4 portions broiler chicken: salt and pepper

Wash the chicken and dry on paper towels. Season well.

½ oz butter (1 Tbs or 15 g): 1 clove garlic, peeled: 3 Tbs olive oil

Heat these in a frying pan and then brown the chicken in it on both sides, about 10 mins.

1 tsp chopped rosemary

Sprinkle this over the chicken.

⅛ pt water (¼ c or ¾ dl)

Gradually add this to the chicken. Cover the pan and simmer gently for 25 mins or until the chicken is tender, adding more water if needed. This cooking can be done in a slow oven, E 325°, G 3.

If there is no lid for the pan use a piece of foil instead. Remove garlic before serving, or earlier if only a mild flavour is required.

CHICKEN SAUTÉ

COOKING TIME: 45 mins: QUANTITIES for 4

4 pieces frying chicken: flour

Wash and dry the chicken and coat it with flour.

Butter or oil

Heat this in a sauté pan or shallow saucepan and fry the chicken until brown. Lift out chicken and pour off any surplus fat. Return chicken to pan.

⅛ pt red wine (¼ c or ¾ dl): ½ Tbs dried onion: 2 oz sliced mushrooms (60 g): Salt and pepper: 1 Tbs chopped green pepper: 2 tomatoes, sliced: 1 rasher bacon, chopped

Add to the chicken, cover and simmer for 30 mins or until tender.

STEAMED CHICKEN

COOKING TIME: ½ hr for pieces and 1–3 hrs for a whole chicken depending on size and age.

QUANTITIES: allow 8 oz per person (250 g)

Prepare as for boiling (see page 109) and cook in the steamer above rapidly boiling water. About ½ hr before the end of cooking, potatoes or noodles may be boiled in the pan below the steamer. Use some of the cooking liquid to add to the sauce. Sauces and accompaniments as for boiled chicken.

CHAPTER FOURTEEN

Quick Vegetable Cooking

THERE are plenty of ready-prepared vegetables to choose from, many of them superior to the "fresh" vegetables on sale. Vegetables are important in the average diet for their vitamin C content but not all pre-prepared vegetables have been processed to retain this vitamin. The best are frozen spinach, broccoli and sprouts and freeze dried cabbage and sprouts. If you use a lot of processed vegetables it is wise to see that plenty of fresh fruit is also included in the diet as this is the alternative source of vitamin C. For tips on buying and storing vegetables, see pages 31 and 34–5.

The most time-consuming part of vegetable cookery is the preparation. For root vegetables this can be reduced by using a mechanical potato peeler. For other vegetables use frozen or freeze dried ones when time-saving is important.

QUICK METHODS OF BOILING FRESH VEGETABLES

(1) Pressure cooking is the quickest of all but, except with vegetables normally requiring 20 minutes or more to cook, the saving with

pressure cooking is small and the timing needs to be precise to avoid over-cooking and spoilage.

(2) Putting vegetables in a small amount (about ½ in or 1 cm) of boiling salted water is the best way for most. If the vegetables are first cut in small pieces (e.g. shred cabbage coarsely, break cauliflower in sprigs), the cooking time required will not be more than 10–15 mins. The lid must be kept on the pan to speed up the cooking and prevent the pan from boiling dry. Drain off any water left and toss the vegetables in a little butter or margarine.

COOKING IN FAT OR OIL

Many vegetables are delicious cooked in a little fat or oil, either in a pan on top of the stove or in a casserole in a moderate oven. Unless the vegetables are small young ones, they should be cut in pieces. Heat just enough fat or oil to cover the bottom of the cooking vessel, add the vegetables, season with salt and pepper, cover and cook gently until tender. A gentle heat is essential to prevent burning and the method is ideal for the new automatically controlled boiling plates or those with reliable control at low settings.

ROASTING OR BAKING IN THE OVEN

This is an ideal method for use with the automatic oven control. Simply brush the prepared vegetables with oil, put them in a baking dish and cook until tender, the time depending on the heat of the oven; see notes with individual vegetables.

SAUCES TO SERVE WITH VEGETABLES

The simplest is to thicken the cooking liquid or the liquid from the can. If you keep a stock of ready-made roux, as recommended on page 54, this can be used for thickening. It is usually better to remove the cooked vegetables and keep them hot while the liquid is thickened. For canned vegetables (except dyed peas), thicken the liquid and then heat the vegetables in this sauce. Chopped parsley and other herbs, grated cheese and other flavourings can also be added to taste.

For an alternative cheese sauce use a ready-made canned one or the quick recipe on page 58.

For a white sauce use Béchamel sauce, recipe page 56 or 63.

Other suitable sauces are: mustard, page 62. Hollandaise, page 60. See also the list of ready prepared sauces, page 53.

ADVANCE PREPARATION OF VEGETABLES AND STORAGE

Apart from washing, drying and storing in polythene bags in the refrigerator, advance preparation of vegetables, especially those providing vitamin C, should be avoided. Do not COOK in advance and reheat because flavour and vitamin content deteriorate too much. If there is not time to cook vegetables it is better to serve a salad instead or if lack of preparation time is the trouble, use frozen or dehydrated vegetables.

ARTICHOKES: GLOBE. These are the ones which look like a large green thistle head. There is no substitute for fresh cooked whole ones which are, in fact, very quick and easy to prepare as follows:

The artichokes must be fresh and the leaves should be green without any brown tips or horny appearance as this indicates old age and staleness.

They are in season in the summer and should be used as soon as possible after purchase. If to be kept, wash and store in a covered container in the refrigerator.

COOKING TIME: 15–45 mins depending on size and age. 10 mins pressure cooking at 15 lb pressure: QUANTITIES: Allow 1 per person

Cut off the stalks and remove the lowest row of leaves.

Soak the artichokes for an hour in cold water to which salt has been added and 1 Tbs vinegar. This is to draw out any insects lurking in the leaves. Drain upside down.

Put them, stem end down, in a little boiling salted water and boil until an outside leaf pulls off easily when tested. Avoid overcooking or flavour will be lost. Drain upside down squeezing gently to remove some of the water.

Serve hot or cold with French dressing, vinaigrette sauce or hollandaise sauce handed separately.

ARTICHOKE HEARTS. This is the part left when all the leaves and the fibrous choke have been removed. They are available in cans and are usually served as an hors d'oeuvre or in salads. They are also sometimes fried in a little butter or oil and used to garnish meat dishes such as steaks.

ARTICHOKES: JERUSALEM. These look like knobbly potatoes and are only available fresh. They are troublesome to peel but quite easy to cook in the same way as potatoes. They can be served with a white or cheese sauce, cold in salads or hors d'oeuvre, or used to make a cream soup.

ASPARAGUS. Available as fresh, frozen or canned.

Buy only very fresh asparagus as it quickly loses flavour after being cut. Use it up as soon as possible. It is best to buy bundles with even-sized heads which will cook evenly.

Canned asparagus has a very different flavour from the fresh but is a pleasant vegetable and useful for soups, salads, garnishes and hors d'oeuvre.

Frozen asparagus is more like the fresh and has a better appearance and colour than the canned.

BOILED ASPARAGUS

COOKING TIME: 15–30 mins depending on size. Pressure cooking 2–3 mins at 15 lb pressure
QUANTITIES allow 6–8 medium sized pieces per person

Wash the asparagus scrubbing the ends if they are dirty. Place in bundles of about a dozen heads or in portions and tie with white string, keeping the heads level. Trim the white ends to an even length. You will need a deep pan so that the grass can stand upright. Special pans are sold for the purpose. Otherwise use a deep pan with an inverted bowl for a lid to give the extra height. Boil enough water in the pan to cover the thick ends of the grass. Add salt, stand the bundles upright and boil gently until the tips are tender. Do not overcook or the tips will be lost and the flavour poor.

Drain in a colander and serve hot with melted butter or brown

butter sauce or hollandaise sauce. Serve cold with French dressing
or vinaigrette sauce.

AUBERGINES. These are only available fresh. They should be firm
to the touch, with an unwrinkled skin. Stale aubergines are practically tasteless. The simplest ways of cooking are grilling or stewing.

To Grill Peel and cut in ½ in (1 cm) slices. Put in the bottom of
an oiled grill pan and cook for 6–8 mins or until tender. Turn once
during cooking. Serve with a sprinkling of grated cheese. They
may be grilled on skewers as part of a kebab.

To Stew Peel and slice and stew in a tomato sauce until tender,
about 20 mins.

BROAD BEANS. Fresh broad beans have the best flavour and they
do not take many minutes to shell. Test one or two pods before
buying them to see they are well filled. Young beans are the nicest
but old ones have a good flavour and if the skins are too thick to
eat the cooked beans may be sieved for a purée. This, of course, is
time-consuming, so most people prefer to use frozen ones instead.
They are of good appearance but tend to be rather tasteless.
Canned ones have a better flavour but do not look so good. To
serve canned ones, thicken the liquid with a roux and heat the beans
in this sauce.

BOILED BROAD BEANS

COOKING TIME 10–40 mins depending on size and age. Pressure
cooking at 15 lb pressure, 2–3 mins or longer if the beans are old:
QUANTITIES: Allow 1–2 lb (½–1 kg) per person, unpodded

Shell the beans. Boil 1 in (2½ cm) of water in a pan and add 1 tsp
salt for every four portions. Add the beans, cover and boil gently
until they are tender. Drain, keeping the liquid for a sauce. Add
some milk to the liquid and thicken it with roux. Add chopped
parsley or savory. Alternatively, instead of making a sauce, toss the
beans in a little butter or margarine and sprinkle with chopped
parsley or savory. A packet parsley sauce could be used, making it
up with some milk and some vegetable water.

Boiled beans may also be served cold in salads or hors d'oeuvre.

BUTTER BEANS. These are available dried or canned. Most busy cooks prefer to use the canned ones but the dried ones are quite simple to cook, either in the pressure cooker or in a casserole in the oven. Some forethought is necessary as the dried beans are best soaked overnight in hot water, or at least for an hour or two. Drain from the soaking water and cook in 1 pt (½ l) water for every 4 oz (125 g) beans. For extra flavour add an onion stuck with a few cloves or use a few bacon rinds.

COOKING TIME 2–3 hrs. Pressure cooking 15–20 mins at 15 lb pressure

They may be served hot with a parsley or tomato sauce or cold with French dressing.

FRENCH BEANS. Fresh are undoubtedly the best but it is difficult to buy good ones. They should not show any signs of the beans inside or they will probably be stringy. Preparation is easy, simply washing and then topping and tailing.

Whole frozen beans or haricots verts are pleasant when fresh are unobtainable but those sold sliced have lost most of their flavour.

Canned French beans have not a very good colour or flavour. They are best when not heated but used in salads.

COOKING TIME: 15–20 mins: QUANTITIES allow 6–8 oz (200–250 g) per person. Pressure cooking 3 mins at 15 lb pressure

Boil about 1 inch (2½ cm) of salted water, add the prepared beans, cover and boil until they are just tender. Avoid overcooking or flavour will be lost. Drain well and toss with a little butter to coat.

If they are to be served cold, simply drain and leave to cool. Then dress with French dressing and garnish with hard-boiled egg.

DRIED HARICOT BEANS. These are small white beans which are cooked in the same way as butter beans. They are used in soups and stews.

RUNNER BEANS. These should be young and flat and show no sign of the bean inside. Many people like to have them sliced very finely and it is possible to buy bean slicers to do this. It is, however, a pity as the beans lose a lot of flavour during cooking. Much better is simply to cut the beans across in about 1 in (2½ cm) lengths.

COOKING TIME: 15–20 mins: QUANTITIES: allow 6–8 oz (200–250 g) per person. Pressure cooking 2–3 mins at 15 lb pressure

Boil 1 in (2½ cm) of water in a saucepan and add 1 tsp salt per lb (½ kg) of beans. Add the beans, cover and boil until they are just tender. Drain and toss with a knob of butter.

Alternatively, drain and leave to cool. Serve as an hors d'oeuvre, dressed with French dressing, or add them to a salad. Hard-boiled eggs and anchovies are good with them.

Sliced runner beans are also available canned, frozen and dehydrated. None of these have the flavour of fresh beans.

BEETROOT. Beetroot is sold ready boiled and this is the simplest way of using it. If you do want to cook your own, pressure cook it whole at 15 lb pressure. Use a pint (½ l) of water and cook for 10–40 mins depending on size and age. It is most commonly used cold for salad or hors d'oeuvre but some like it hot with a white or vinegar sauce. Remove skin before slicing or dicing according to taste.

It is also sold sliced in vinegar in jars or sliced or small whole beets are sold in cans. It is a good idea to stock some of each of these as a reserve.

BROCCOLI. This is sold in three different forms. The first looks like a cauliflower and is used in the same way. The second called Calabrese is like a small green cauliflower on a stalk and is cooked like cauliflower, while the third is known as sprouting broccoli and consists of green or purple heads like cauliflower sprigs on a stalk.

They are cooked like any green vegetable.

Frozen sprouting broccoli is very good, better than much sold fresh which is too often over-mature and inclined to be tough and stringy.

BRUSSELS SPROUTS. These are available fresh, frozen and dehydrated. Poor quality fresh ones take a long time to prepare because they need to be inspected individually and trimmed of old leaves. Good quality ones simply need to be washed.

To speed up the cooking, cut a cross in the base of large ones. The very best fresh ones are the small variety of even size but they are not often generally available. Good quality frozen and dehydrated ones can be very palatable. Finely shredded raw sprouts make an excellent winter salad.

Cook fresh ones in the same way as any green vegetable and toss with butter before serving.

COOKING TIME: about 15 mins:
QUANTITIES allow 6–8 oz (200–250 g) per person. Pressure cooking 3–4 mins at 15 lb pressure

CABBAGE. Green cabbage is sold either fresh or dehydrated. White cabbage is sold by delicatessens as cole slaw salad and as sauerkraut, the latter also being canned. Red cabbage is sold fresh, pickled in vinegar or canned, cooked with apple, onion and spices and ready for heating and serving as a vegetable with meat.

BOILED CABBAGE

COOKING TIME: 10–15 mins
QUANTITIES: allow 4–6 oz (125–200 g) per person

Wash the cabbage and slice it into about ½ inch pieces. Boil ½ inch (1 cm) water, add salt and cabbage, cover with a lid and boil until just tender but not mushy. Drain and toss with a little butter. Season with pepper and serve.

RED CABBAGE. This is better freshly cooked than from a tin and is not time-consuming provided you have a mechanical shredder. It does not need any attention during cooking. It can be done on top or in the oven.

COOKING TIME: ½–¾ hr: QUANTITIES for 4
1 *lb red cabbage* (½ *kg): 1 large apple: 1 large onion*

Wash the cabbage, cut it in quarters and remove the hard centre stalk. Skin the onion and peel and core the apple. Put all these in the shredder to give about ¼ inch (½ cm) slices. Put in pan or casserole.

> 1 oz dripping or lard (2 Tbs or 30 g): 2 Tbs stock or water: 2 Tbs
> vinegar: 1 tsp salt: Pinch of pepper: 1 Tbs brown sugar

Add these to the cabbage, cover and boil gently until just tender. There should be hardly any liquid left when cooking is finished. It is very good served with roast pork or pork chops or sausages.

SAUERKRAUT. The canned variety is simply heated. That sold loose is usually raw and needs to be boiled in a little water for about 2 hrs. Alternatively, it can be stewed with a little white wine and butter.

CARROTS. Small young carrots are the quickest to prepare as they merely need to be washed, the tops trimmed and then be cooked whole in a little boiling salted water. Old carrots need to be peeled and sliced and will then cook quickly too.

COOKING TIME: about 20 mins
Pressure cooking 2–10 mins at 15 lb pressure; the longer time being for whole old carrots
QUANTITIES: allow 6–8 oz (200–250 g) per person

When they are tender but not soft, drain and toss in butter, or serve with a parsley sauce using the cooking liquid plus some milk to make it.

CANNED CARROTS. Use the liquid to make a sauce and heat the carrots gently in this. Alternatively, heat the drained carrots in a little melted butter.

DRIED CARROTS. Cook according to instructions on the packet.

CAULIFLOWER. Available fresh or frozen. It is easily prepared and cooks quickly.

COOKING TIME: 15–20 mins. Pressure cooking at 15 lb pressure, 3 mins for sprigs, 5–6 mins if whole

The best way of cooking it is to cut it into sprigs, wash quickly and put in a little boiling salted water with the lid on the pan. Cook until just tender. It has a better flavour if it is still firm. Drain and serve plain with a little melted butter poured over it or serve with a white or cheese sauce.

CELERY. Available fresh or canned. The best way of serving fresh celery is raw to eat with cheese or sliced in salads. If it is wanted for a hot vegetable, cut it in pieces about 2 in (5 cm) long and boil in a little salted water.

Drain and serve with a little butter or with a white or cheese sauce.

CARROTS AND CELERY

COOKING TIME: about 20 mins: QUANTITIES for 4

3–4 medium sized carrots: 4–5 large sticks celery

Scrape and slice the carrots. Scrub and slice the celery.

Cook them together with a little boiling salted water until they are tender. Drain.

Pinch sugar: 1 Tbs chopped parsley: 1 oz butter or margarine (2 Tbs or 30 g)

Add to the hot vegetables, toss well and serve.

CELERY AND MUSTARD SAUCE

COOKING TIME: about ½ hr: QUANTITIES for 4
1 lb celery (½ kg)

Scrub celery and cut in 1 in pieces. Boil until tender in a little salted water. Drain and keep hot.

2 oz butter (4 Tbs or 60 g): 1 tsp made mustard: Pepper

Melt these together, add the hot celery and mix well before serving.

CHICORY. This is one of the easiest vegetables to use because it needs no preparation apart from rinsing in cold water. For salads it can be sliced or separated into leaves and mixed with other ingredients.

The simplest way of cooking is to boil the pieces for about 20 mins in a little salted water to which has been added a few drops of lemon juice. When it is tender, drain well and serve plain or chop it and mix with a little melted butter and a pinch of sugar.

It can also be cooked in a casserole in the oven with a little water, butter, seasoning and lemon juice. Time about 45 mins.

CORN. Sold as fresh corn-on-the-cob or frozen and also as canned corn and loose, frozen corn. Fresh corn is cooked as follows:

COOKING TIME: 10–12 mins: QUANTITIES: allow 1 ear per person: Pressure cooking 4 mins at 15 lb pressure

Remove the leafy sheath and the 'silk' from round the corn grains. Rinse in cold water and boil in a small amount of salted water until tender. Drain and serve with plenty of melted butter.

Alternatively, strip the corn off the cooked ears with a fork and re-heat with a little melted butter.

Corn may also be served with a Béchamel sauce and this is the best way of using canned corn.

COURGETTES. These are baby marrows about 3–4 ins (8–10 cm) long.

Wash them in cold water and put them in a pan or casserole with a little butter, salt and pepper. Cover and cook gently for about 15 mins.

Serve with the cooking liquid.

CUCUMBER. When these are plentiful and cheap they make a delicious and quickly cooked vegetable. Simply wash them and cut in about ½ in (1 cm) dice. Put in a pan or casserole with a little butter and seasoning, cover and stew gently until tender. They may also be fried in a little butter.

LEEKS. These are usually only available fresh. Many people avoid them because they think they are troublesome to prepare but this is not so. The best way is to trim off the roots but not so much that the leek will fall apart. Trim off all except the bottom 2 in (5 cm) of the green part. Slice the leek almost down to the root end and wash under a running cold tap, separating the tops of the leaves with your thumbs to allow all dirt to wash away. Drain upside down.

COOKING TIME: 10–20 mins: QUANTITIES allow 1–2 leeks per person. Pressure cooking 3 mins at 15 lb pressure

Use a pan large enough to let them lie flat. Boil ½ in (1 cm) salted water, add the leeks, cover and boil until they are just tender at the root ends. Drain in a colander and serve plain or with a little melted butter or a Béchamel or cheese sauce.

They are also used as a salad: see page 144.

MUSHROOMS. Cultivated mushrooms do not need to be peeled or have the stalks removed. Simply rinse in cold water and drain. They may be baked, boiled, fried or grilled.

QUANTITIES: Allow 1–2 oz (30–60 g) per person
COOKING TIME: about 10 mins: TEMPERATURE: E 375°, G 5

To Bake Grease a shallow baking dish generously with butter. Put in the mushrooms, season with salt and pepper, cover with a lid or with foil and bake until they are just tender. Serve with any liquid in the dish.

To Boil for garnishing. Put in a pan with white stock or water and lemon juice and simmer for about 8 mins. Drain and serve.

To Fry Fry in hot butter, oil or bacon fat until they are just tender. Avoid overcooking or flavour is lost.

To Grill Put on the grill rack, brush with oil and grill until just tender. They may also be threaded on skewers with a kebab.

CANNED MUSHROOMS. Many different kinds are available, the most useful being mushrooms for grilling or frying and those for flavouring stews and other savoury dishes.

DRIED MUSHROOMS. These are most suitable to use for flavouring stews and casseroles or in soups.

ONIONS. The only alternative to fresh onions or those pickled in vinegar is to use dehydrated flakes or onion salt. Dehydrated onions are very useful where small amounts of chopped onions are needed for flavouring. Where only a small amount of flavour is wanted the salt is ideal.

For sliced or chopped fresh onions there are covered choppers available which very much help to prevent the irritating volatile substances from reaching the eyes.

The simplest way of preparing onions to serve as a vegetable is to bake them in their skins. Simply wash them and wrap each one in foil. Stand them on a baking tin and cook in a moderate oven until they feel soft when squeezed, about 45–60 mins. Either serve them in the foil or remove the outer skins and serve with a little butter.

Peeled onions can either be baked in a little fat or boiled. To boil they will take ½–1 or more hours depending on the size, or 3–10 minutes in the pressure cooker at 15 lb pressure.

PARSNIPS. Available either fresh or canned. If you buy only washed, firm, even-shaped ones, they are no more troublesome to prepare than a potato. Use a potato peeler to remove a thin layer of outer skin and cut off the top where the leaves have been. If they are to be prepared in advance, store them in a polythene bag in the refrigerator.

QUANTITIES: Allow 6–8 oz (200–250 g) per person

To Boil

COOKING TIME: 15–30 mins depending on size and age. Pressure cooking 3–8 mins at 15 lb pressure

Cooking is speeded up if the parsnips are cut in halves or in chunks or slices. Put them in about ½ in (1 cm) of boiling salted water and cook with the lid on the pan until they are just tender. Avoid overcooking as this makes them watery and unpleasant. Drain and toss with a little butter or mash with butter and pepper.

To Bake or Roast

COOKING TIME: ½ hr or more depending on size and temperature of oven

TEMPERATURE: E 350°, G 4 or use a higher temperature, as convenient

Cut parsnips in halves or quarters, roll in oil or melted fat in a baking tin and cook until tender. Alternatively, they may be cooked round a joint.

To Stew in Butter (or other fat or oil) Cut in slices about ½–1 in (1–2 cm) thick. Heat enough fat or oil to cover the bottom of the pan, add the parsnips, season, cover and cook gently until they are tender. Shake the pan or stir occasionally to turn them over. For the best flavour allow them to brown lightly.

PEAS. Shelling peas is a very time-consuming job, especially when, as so often happens, the pods are not well filled and so many have to be opened to produce enough peas.

The best alternatives are either, when fresh peas are in season, buy them from a shop which sells them ready shelled, or use frozen peas.

Dehydrated peas are a good alternative and imported canned garden peas are of good flavour though not such good appearance as the others. Home produced canned garden and processed peas are usually coloured artificially but are cheap and popular.

BOILED FRESH PEAS

COOKING TIME: 15–20 mins depending on size and age. Pressure cooking 1–2 mins at 15 lb pressure:

QUANTITIES: Allow at least ½ lb (250 g) unshelled per person; shelled allow 3–4oz (100–125 g) per person

Boil ½ in (1 cm) water in a pan with a little salt and sugar. Add the peas, cover and boil gently until they are just tender. Drain and toss the peas with a knob of butter.

SWEET PEPPERS. Fresh peppers may be green, red or yellow, but are most frequently green.

Red and yellow ones are available pickled and canned. Both the fresh and the canned ones are used for garnishing and flavouring purposes and in salads, see page 143.

Fresh ones are also stuffed and baked.

Fresh Sweet Peppers When in good condition, sweet peppers have a smooth, shiny skin and are firm, with no soft patches. Wash and cut them in half and remove all the small, white seeds. Cut out the white pithy parts too.

To Sauté Cook prepared halves of peppers in a little oil until they are tender.

Use as a garnish for grills.

STUFFED GREEN PEPPERS

COOKING TIME: 20 mins: QUANTITIES for 4

4 green peppers

Cut the peppers in half lengthwise and remove all the seeds, rinsing under the cold tap. Put peppers in a little boiling salted water and boil for 15–20 mins. Drain.

About 8 oz can of filling: suitable ones are risotto, chicken in a sauce, meat in a sauce, macaroni cheese, spaghetti in a sauce, chicken and rice, prawns and rice, minced steak

While the peppers are cooking, heat the filling.

Put the cooked drained pepper halves in the grill pan or an oven dish and add the filling.

Browned crumbs

Cover the top of the filling with a layer of crumbs and brown under the grill or in the top of a hot oven. Serve plain or with a sauce such as :

Tomato sauce

ALTERNATIVE METHOD Put the cold filling in raw pepper halves and put in a baking dish. Add a little water, stock or tomato sauce to moisten the dish. Put a little butter or oil on top of each and bake for 45 mins at E 375° G 5.

PEAS WITH PEPPERS

COOKING TIME: 5–10 mins: QUANTITIES for 4

1 *lb frozen or canned peas* (½ *kg*)

Boil frozen peas for 3 mins. Drain and keep hot. Heat canned peas in their own liquor, drain and keep hot.

1 *oz butter* (2 *Tbs or* 30 *g*)

Heat in a pan and allow to brown

½ *a fresh or frozen green or red pepper, chopped: Salt and pepper*

Add chopped pepper to the butter and cook for a few minutes. Add the peas, season to taste and serve when well heated.

POTATOES. If your family is fond of potatoes, it will pay you to invest in a mechanical potato peeler. When new potatoes are in season, encourage the family to like boiled ones served 'au naturel', that is, in their skins. The skins are very thin and add greatly to the flavour. Baked jacket potatoes are another time saver.

For quick mashed potatoes, the packets of powder and flakes are useful and palatable if you add milk and butter and use them as soon as they are prepared.

Other ready-prepared varieties available are canned whole potatoes and frozen ones either mashed, croquettes or chips.

BAKED JACKET POTATOES

COOKING TIME: 45 mins or longer, depending on size
QUANTITIES: Allow 1 medium to large potato per portion
TEMPERATURE E 400–450°, 6–8

Potatoes can be baked at lower temperatures for very much longer times but then they do not have the tasty skins and floury insides of those baked faster. Choose potatoes without blemish and scrub well. Dry them in paper towels and brush the skins with oil. This is not essential but it makes the skins taste better. Put on a baking shelf or oven grid and bake until they feel soft when squeezed gently in a cloth. They should then be pricked to let the steam out and keep them floury, otherwise they become soggy as they cool. Prick a cross on top of each, using a table fork and gently squeeze from the bottom to make the pricked bit open.

Add a knob of butter and some seasoning and serve.

BOILED POTATOES

COOKING TIME: 20–40 mins depending on size and condition.
Pressure cooking 4–12 mins at 15 lb pressure:
QUANTITIES Allow 5–8 oz (150–250 g) or more per person

To cook evenly, potatoes should be of uniform size so cut big ones to match the smaller ones. Either scrub and cook in their jackets or peel thinly. New potatoes are usually scraped instead of peeling but this depends on how fresh they are.

Put 2 inches of water in a pan with 1 tsp salt to each pound of potatoes. Boil the water before adding the potatoes, put on the lid and cook gently until they are almost tender when tested with a fork. Do not boil rapidly as this encourages them to break. Drain away the water, return potatoes to the pan and put in a warm place with the lid tilted to allow them to dry off and become floury.

MASHED POTATOES. Boil as above and then mash or put through a potato ricer. Return to the pan and add 1 Tbs milk and 1 oz butter (30 g) per pound of potatoes. Beat well until smooth and creamy. Do this over a gentle heat to make sure the potatoes do not cool too much. An electric beater can be used for the creaming. If a soft purée is wanted, add more milk.

ROAST POTATOES. This can be done at varying temperatures to fit in with other things being cooked at the same time but quick cooking usually gives best results.

Quick method

COOKING TIME: 45 mins: TEMPERATURE E 450°, G 8

Peel the potatoes and roll them in flour. Heat some fat or oil in a baking tin and roll the potatoes in it. Put near the top of the oven and turn once during cooking.

Alternatively, brush the unfloured potatoes with oil and cook as before or put round the joint. If the meat is being cooked at a low temperature, it is better to put the potatoes in a separate tin near the top of the oven and allow 1–2 hours for cooking.

SAUTÉ POTATOES. Use boiled or drained canned potatoes for this. Make sure canned ones are well drained otherwise the moisture will make the fat splash. Cut the potatoes in thick slices. Heat enough oil or fat to cover the bottom of the frying pan and when it is hot add the potatoes in a single layer, season and fry until brown on both sides. Serve at once.

PUMPKIN. This is available fresh or as canned purée. The fresh is only in season for a short time. Baking is the best method of cooking it.

COOKING TIME 45–60 mins: TEMPERATURE E 375–400° G 5–6

Cut the pumpkin into pieces each of about 4 oz. Remove seeds and pith but do not peel. Put peel side down in a baking dish and brush with oil. Bake until tender.

Pumpkin pieces may also be cooked round a joint.

TURNIPS. These are usually sold fresh, though there are some canned ones available. Older ones are used for flavouring purposes and the young ones in summertime are used as a vegetable or grated raw in salads.

Very young small turnips are simply washed but older ones need to be peeled thickly to remove the outer skin.

To Boil

COOKING TIME: 15–20 mins:

Pressure cooking 4–5 mins at 15 lb pressure

Leave small ones whole but cut large ones in thick slices or dice them. Put them in ½ in (1 cm) boiling salted water and cook until tender. Drain and mash with butter and pepper.

TURNIPS COOKED IN BUTTER. Prepare the turnips and cut them in small pieces or leave very small ones whole. Melt enough butter to cover the bottom of the saucepan. Add the turnips, season, and cover the pan. Cook gently until they are tender. Serve with any liquid in the pan.

VEGETABLE MARROW. These are best when they are small and young, not more than about 9 in (23 cm) long. Simply wash them, cut into pieces leaving the skin on and the centre in. Either boil them in a little salted water or cook in a little butter until they are tender.

Pieces of larger marrow are peeled and have the seeds and pulp removed and can then either be boiled, stewed in fat or baked in the oven with a little fat, or round the joint.

Cubes of marrow are also good stewed with tomatoes and a little chopped or dehydrated onion.

VEGETABLES AU GRATIN

COOKING TIME: ½ hr: QUANTITIES for 4
1–1 ½ *lb vegetables (500–750 g)*: ½ *pt* (¼ *l*) *cheese sauce, canned or quick recipe, page* 58: *dried breadcrumbs*

Best vegetables are: cauliflower, leeks, onions, celery, cabbage, sprouts, chicory and vegetable marrow. Use fresh, canned or frozen.

. Boil the raw or frozen vegetables, heat canned, and make or heat the sauce. Heat a flat oven-proof dish and put the hot, drained vegetables in it. Pour the sauce over the top and sprinkle thickly with brown crumbs. Put under the grill to brown the top lightly and serve at once.

CHAPTER FIFTEEN

Salads for Any Occasion

SALADS are a wonderful aid to the busy woman. They can find a place in so many meals and, if a good store of suitable ingredients is always kept available, they can be assembled in minutes.

Salads can be served as a first course, as part of hors d'oeuvre, or in place of it. They are an accepted accompaniment to cold meats but many people enjoy the temperature and texture contrast of serving cold salad with hot meat. Many will be familiar with this custom from continental holidays. Certain salads have traditionally been served with hot meats in English cookery, for example, orange salad with duck. Serving salads in place of a cooked vegetable is an obvious saving for the busy woman, provided, of course, that the lettuce and other salad vegetables are kept washed and ready to use from the refrigerator.

Other ways of serving salad are as a course to follow the meat and sometimes to accompany cheese in place of a sweet. Salads containing meat, fish, eggs or cheese make excellent main dishes for lunch, high tea or supper meals. A soup and salad meal appeals at any time of the year.

SALAD INGREDIENTS
RAW VEGETABLES
One or other of these is the basis of all salads—a 'salad' being something made with raw vegetables, either alone or with other ingredients. They should always be fresh and crisp so preparation and storage are very important.

Brussels sprouts make an excellent winter salad. Keep some washed, drained and in a covered dish in the refrigerator. To use, either slice finely with a sharp knife or put in a vegetable slicer. Use French dressing or mayonnaise.

Cabbage This needs to be the tender heart of cabbage. Wash, drain and store in the refrigerator. Slice with a sharp knife as finely as possibly or use a vegetable shredder. Best dressed with a salad cream or mayonnaise.

Carrot Store washed ones in the refrigerator and either grate or shred when required. Especially useful for garnishing and mixing with other ingredients.

Cauliflower Wash and store in the refrigerator. Only the flower heads are used raw, either whole or sliced. They are usually mixed with other ingredients.

Chicory is used alone or with other ingredients. It keeps very well if washed, drained and stored in a covered dish in the refrigerator. The leaves may be separated and used whole, alone or with other vegetables or the heads may be sliced coarsely or finely according to taste. Any kind of dressing is suitable.

Celery This too keeps well in the refrigerator but must be fresh and crisp when it is put in. When served with cheese, the stalks are left whole but in mixed salads it is usually sliced fairly finely. The small inner stalks are sometimes used as a garnish for mixed salads.

Cucumber This too can be kept crisp if stored in a box or polythene bag in the refrigerator. It may be used peeled or unpeeled and sliced, diced or cut in sticks. French dressing is usually considered the best especially for a salad of cucumber alone.

Endive This is used in the same way as lettuce and keeps very well in the refrigerator. It is very good as a basis for mixed salads or by itself.

Lettuce The most popular salad to serve with hot meat and for a basis for other ingredients. Lettuce can be washed, drained and stored in a covered dish in the refrigerator. It will keep for up to a week, the time depending on the variety. A fairly robust, crisp lettuce keeps longest. A delicate, hot-house lettuce which bruises easily will usually only keep in good condition for 2–3 days. The long or cos lettuce is the best for keeping. Lettuce has the best flavour if the leaves are left whole or torn coarsely, but coarse outer leaves are sometimes better shredded. French dressing is the best for plain lettuce salads.

Mustard and Cress is a fairly delicate vegetable and does not keep very long. It is usually used for garnishing purposes.

Onions For the most delicate flavour, use chopped chives; for more robust salads, spring onions or sliced ordinary onions are used, the large mild ones being the best.

Radishes are best used for garnishing or by themselves with cheese or with sausage as an hors d'oeuvre. Washed and drained they keep well in the refrigerator.

Spinach This keeps well in the refrigerator. It is usually better in a mixed salad where only a few finely shredded leaves are used.

Turnips Only young, crisp ones are suitable for salads and they are usually mixed with other ingredients. They are best grated or shredded, after peeling.

Watercress Another vegetable favoured as an accompaniment for hot meat, usually as a garnish. Watercress will keep in the refrigerator but for only 2–3 days in prime condition. It can be used in a salad alone, dressed with French dressing or mixed with other ingredients. It is usually left in sprigs.

COOKED VEGETABLES

Any vegetables, cooked or canned may be added to mixed salads. They should be well drained and mixed with either French or a thick dressing. Either dressed or plain ones can be stored in a covered dish in the refrigerator.

FRUITS

Any fresh, cooked, canned or dried fruits may be used. Among the best are bananas, pineapple, pears, raw plums, prunes, apples, raisins, grapes, dates, tomatoes and citrus fruits.

MEAT AND FISH

Any kind, fresh or canned. Once it has been prepared and dressed, store it in the refrigerator and use up the same day.

EGGS

Always keep a few hard-boiled eggs in the refrigerator for quick salads and for garnishing. Scrambled eggs also make a pleasant salad when mixed with dressing and put in a nest of salad greens.

CHEESE

Any kind is suitable, in pieces, grated or diced. Crumbly cheeses like blue are sometimes added to the dressing.

FLAVOURINGS

Use any fresh herbs, spring onions, chives, garlic, gherkins, olives, pickles, sweet peppers. Most people prefer not to have pieces of garlic in a salad but to have the bowl rubbed with a cut clove before the salad is put in.

SALAD DRESSINGS. See Sauces, pages 63–4.

Useful canned vegetables to keep for salads

Asparagus	Sliced mushrooms
Baked Beans	Peas
Beetroot in vinegar or plain	Potato salad

Broad Beans	Green beans
Butter Beans	Vegetable salad
Corn	Artichoke hearts
Macedoine	Sweet peppers

SALADS FOR THE FIRST COURSE (or to serve as a separate course after the main dish in place of a sweet)

BEETROOT AND EGG SALAD

QUANTITIES for 4

2 hard-boiled eggs: 1 lb cooked or canned beetroot (½ kg): French dressing: watercress or mustard and cress

Peel and slice the beetroot or choose sliced, canned. Arrange it on individual plates. Pour a little dressing over it. Shell and slice the eggs and use them as a decoration together with the green stuff.

SHRIMP AND EGG SALAD

QUANTITIES for 4

1 lettuce

Arrange nests of washed and dried lettuce leaves on 4 plates

4 hard-boiled eggs

Shell and cut in half. Place in the lettuce nests.

Mayonnaise or salad cream: chopped chives or parsley

Cover eggs with mayonnaise and garnish with the chopped herbs.

6 oz shelled, canned or frozen shrimps (200 g)

Surround the eggs with the shrimps.

ANCHOVY AND EGG SALAD

QUANTITY for 4

A cut clove of garlic

Rub the salad bowl with this.

2 eggs, hardboiled

Cut in half and remove yolks. Put these through a ricer or small sieve, into the salad bowl. Chop or slice the whites and reserve for decoration.

¼ tsp salt: ½ tsp sugar: 1 tsp dry mustard: pinch of pepper: pinch of paprika pepper

Add to the egg yolks and mix

1 ½ Tbs vinegar: 1 small tin (2 oz or 60 g) anchovy fillets

Mix in the vinegar to make a smooth paste. Drain and chop the anchovies and mix them in.

6 Tbs oil

Stir into the other ingredients.

4–8 outside leaves of lettuce, washed and drained

Shred coarsely and, just before serving, combine gently with the other ingredients. Sprinkle the egg whites over the top.

TOMATO SALAD. Wash and dry the tomatoes and slice them. Dress with French dressing containing a good pinch of sugar or sprinkle the tomatoes with sugar before dressing. Sprinkle the salad with chopped parsley or tarragon. Alternatively, use tarragon vinegar to make the dressing.

TOMATO AND SWEET PEPPER SALAD. Mix the tomatoes with an equal quantity of sliced, canned, red peppers, well drained.

SWEET PEPPER SALAD. Wash the peppers, cut in half and remove all seeds and pith. Slice them finely and dress with French dressing. Add a little chopped onion or chives.

CUCUMBER AND TOMATO SALAD. Make in the same way as tomato salad but use equal amounts of sliced cucumber and sliced tomato.

EGG MAYONNAISE. Allow one hard-boiled egg per person. Cut in half lengthwise and arrange on a bed of salad greens. Mask the egg with mayonnaise and decorate with paprika pepper or a little tomato or canned red pepper or other garnish to taste.

LOBSTER MAYONNAISE. Use canned, cooked or frozen lobster. Mix it with mayonnaise and arrange individual portions on a bed of salad greens. Garnish with paprika pepper or red or green vegetable, or chopped herbs.

CAULIFLOWER AND ANCHOVY SALAD. Mask cooked, cold cauliflower sprigs with mayonnaise and garnish with canned fillets of anchovy, plain or stuffed.

DRESSED LEEKS (for hors d'oeuvre or salad)

COOKING TIME: 15–20 mins: QUANTITIES for 4
16 *small leeks*

Remove the coarse green tops and cut the leeks in half lengthwise. Wash them thoroughly under running water. Drain well and tie in 4 bundles. Boil in a little salted water until they are just tender. Drain and remove the ties.

4–5 *Tbs French dressing*

Serve the leeks warm or cold with the dressing poured over.

ALTERNATIVE METHOD

2 *hard-boiled eggs: chopped chives and parsley*

Shell and chop the eggs and sprinkle them over the leeks together with the chopped herbs. Serve cold.

SALADS FOR SERVING WITH HOT OR COLD MEAT

LETTUCE SALAD. The lettuce should be washed and dried carefully. Small leaves are left whole but very large ones torn in pieces with the fingers. Put in the salad bowl and pour over it some French dressing tossing the lettuce gently using salad servers or a spoon and fork and just enough dressing to coat the lettuce lightly. Serve at once because allowing it to stand after dressing will make the lettuce become flabby and slimy.

For flavouring, either rub the bowl with a cut clove of garlic before putting the lettuce in, or sprinkle chopped fresh green herbs over the lettuce before or after dressing.

MIXED GREEN SALAD. This is made in the same way as lettuce salad but a mixture of greens is used, for example, some endive, watercress, shredded spinach leaves, mustard and cress, shredded Brussels sprouts, or shredded cabbage heart. Other ingredients can also be added to taste such as leaves of chicory, spring onions, cauliflower sprigs, sliced celery or grated carrot or turnip.

BEETROOT SALAD. See page 142.

SPROUTS AND CELERY SALAD

QUANTITIES according to appetite but about 2–3 sprouts and a stick of celery per person

Raw Brussels sprouts: salad dressing, any kind: crisp sticks of raw celery: sliced hard-boiled egg to garnish

Wash the vegetables thoroughly and dry well. Either slice the sprouts and celery with a sharp knife or use a shredder. Use them in equal quantities and mix in a salad bowl with the dressing to moisten.

Garnish with either egg or beetroot or both.

This salad may be allowed to stand for a short time without spoiling but store it in the refrigerator to keep it crisp.

COLE SLAW. This may be purchased ready made from the delicatessen but is easy to make if you have an efficient vegetable shredder.

Raw white cabbage heart: optional extras, chopped onion or green peppers, sliced hard-boiled egg: mayonnaise or salad cream

Wash and dry the cabbage and make sure it is crisp. Slice it as finely as possible on a shredder or by hand. Put it in a salad bowl and dress liberally with mayonnaise or other similar dressing. It may be served plain or with one of the optional flavourings or garnishes.

The salad may be prepared in advance and stored in a covered dish in the refrigerator.

POTATO SALAD. Available canned, or ready made from the delicatessen.

If you are making your own, use new potatoes or the waxy Dutch kind. Floury potatoes do not make such a good salad but if these are the only ones available, boil them in their skins until the potatoes are just tender then plunge in cold water to stop any further cooking and allow them to become quite cold before peeling and dicing.

QUANTITIES for 4

1 ½ lb boiled potatoes (750 g): 1 Tbs finely chopped onion or chives: ¼ pt mayonnaise or French dressing (½ c or ½ dl): 1 Tbs chopped green herbs

If new or waxy potatoes are used, dress them while they are still warm. Cut the cooked potatoes in cubes and mix with the onion and dressing. When cold, serve with the green herbs sprinkled on top.

This salad can be made in advance and kept in a cool place in a covered dish.

TOMATO SALAD. See page 143.

SWEET PEPPER AND TOMATO SALAD. See page 143.

CHICORY AND BEETROOT SALAD

QUANTITIES for 4

4 small head of chicory: 1 medium sized cooked beetroot, or use canned

Wash and dry the chicory and slice it across in ½ in slices. Skin and dice the beetroot and mix with the chicory.

1 hard-boiled egg: 1 Tbs tarragon vinegar: juice of ½ lemon: salt and pepper: ⅛ pt yoghurt (¼ c or ¾ dl)

Mash the egg yolk and mix it with the other ingredients to make a dressing. Pour it over the salad and decorate with the chopped egg white. This can be kept for a short period in a covered dish in the refrigerator, but is better if freshly mixed.

CUCUMBER SALAD. Whether the cucumber is peeled or not is a matter of taste. The small fat ridge cucumbers available in the late summer make excellent salads but should be peeled. Slice the cucumber as finely as possible and put it in layers in a shallow dish. Pour over a French dressing to which sugar has been added, amount according to taste.

Many like a fairly sweetish cucumber salad.

ORANGE SALAD. The traditional salad to serve with duck but also good with veal, lamb, ham and other cold meats.

QUANTITIES for 4

4 oranges

Peel and remove all pith. Slice into thin rounds, removing any pips.

Chopped fresh tarragon or chervil (optional)

Sprinkle over the orange

2 Tbs olive oil: 2 tsp lemon juice: 1 Tbs vinegar

Mix these and pour them over the oranges. Leave to stand for a while.

Watercress

Serve the salad on individual plates with watercress to garnish.

MAIN DISH SALADS

CHEESE SALAD BOWL

QUANTITIES for 4

1 *cucumber*: 12 *stuffed olives*: 8 *oz cheese* (250 g): *French dressing*: *watercress*

Slice the cucumber and olives. Cube the cheese. Wash and dry the watercress. Combine cucumber, cheese, olives and dressing and serve on a bed of watercress.

CHICKEN AND CUCUMBER SALAD

QUANTITIES for 4

8 *oz diced cooked chicken* (1 *c or* 250 *g*): 8 *oz cooked or canned green peas* (1 *c or* 250 *g*): *salad dressing to choice*: 8 *oz coarsely chopped walnuts* (1 *c or* 250 *g*): 1 *medium cucumber, diced*

Combine all the ingredients with enough dressing to moisten.

Lettuce

Arrange washed and dried lettuce leaves to line the bowl or make individual nests on serving plates and arrange the salad mixture in the centre.

Tomato or paprika pepper to garnish

CAULIFLOWER AND BLUE CHEESE SALAD

QUANTITIES for 4

4 *oz cauliflower* (125 *g*) (*flower only*): 8 *stuffed olives*: 4 *spring onions*

Wash and drain the cauliflower and onions. Slice them and the olives.

4 Tbs French dressing

Mix with the vegetables.

1 small head of lettuce or other salad greens, washed and drained

Just before serving, tear the lettuce in pieces and mix it into the salad.

2–3 oz blue cheese (60–100 g)

Crumble this over the top of the salad and serve at once.

CHEESE AND CUCUMBER SALAD

QUANTITIES for 4

8 oz firm cheese, diced (250 g): 8 oz cucumber, diced (250 g): 1 Tbs lemon juice or vinegar: ½ tsp salt: Pinch of pepper: ½ tsp dry mustard

Mix the seasonings and lemon or vinegar together and toss the cheese and cucumber in it.

1 lettuce: 4 tomatoes

Wash and drain the vegetables.
Put the salad in a nest of lettuce leaves and garnish with the sliced tomato.

CURRY SALAD

QUANTITIES for 4–6

8 oz cold chicken or other meat (250 g): 8 oz can diced carrot (250 g): ½ tsp chopped or grated onion: 2 apples: 3 hard-boiled eggs

Peel and chop the apples, shell and chop the eggs coarsely, or slice them. Mix all ingredients together.

8 Tbs mayonnaise: 1 Tbs curry powder: salt to taste

Combine these and add to the meat mixture, combining gently and thoroughly.

Lettuce leaves

Line a salad bowl with washed and dried lettuce leaves or put individual portions on plates. Add the salad and garnish with a slice of the egg or other decoration to taste.

SALMON MAYONNAISE. This can be made with fresh, frozen or canned salmon. Fresh salmon is best boiled; frozen cutlets cooked en papilotte, see page 84.

QUANTITIES for 4

1 *lettuce: mayonnaise: chopped parsley: 8 oz cooked or canned salmon (250 g): 1 small beetroot or 3–4 tomatoes: 1 hard-boiled egg*

Wash and dry the lettuce and arrange individual portions in a nest on each plate. Put the portion of salmon in the centre, mask with mayonnaise, and garnish with egg and the vegetables.

BOILED BEEF SALAD. Can also be made with other cooked meats.

QUANTITIES for 4

12 *oz cold boiled beef (375 g): 1 lb boiled waxy or new potatoes (½ kg): 4 hard-boiled eggs*

Have the meat thinly sliced and arrange it on a platter with slices of potato and egg.

Chopped chives and parsley: French dressing

Sprinkle the salad liberally with the herbs and dressing.

FISH SALAD. Use any cold fish, steamed or boiled. Serve either in pieces as for Salmon Mayonnaise or flake the fish and mix with dressing.

ROLL MOP SALAD. Roll mop pickled herrings can be purchased singly from the delicatessen or in jars.

1 *roll mop per person: potato salad: lettuce:* 1 *slice brown bread and butter per person: tomatoes*

Arrange a nest of lettuce leaves on each plate and put a slice of bread and butter in the middle. Put the roll mop on this with a little potato salad at one end and quartered or sliced tomatoes at the other end.

CRAB SALAD

QUANTITIES for 4

8 *oz crab meat, canned, fresh or frozen* (250 *g*): 4 *Brussels sprouts:* 1 *small carrot: a quarter of a curled endive:* 1 *tomato:* 2 *sticks celery: French dressing or other type as liked*

Wash and dry the vegetables, shred the sprouts, slice the tomato and celery. Grate the carrot and chop the endive coarsely. Combine all the ingredients with enough dressing to moisten.

TONGUE SALAD

QUANTITIES for 4

6 *oz cooked or canned tongue* (200 *g*): 4 *hard-boiled eggs:* 1 *medium size beetroot:* 1 *apple*

Skin the beetroot and apple and cut all the ingredients into small pieces reserving two of the egg yolks for dressing.

Pinch of pepper: ½ *tsp salt:* ½ *tsp mustard:* 2 *Tbs vinegar:* 2 *Tbs single cream or evaporated milk*

Mash the egg yolks and seasoning and mix smoothly with first the vinegar and then the cream. Mix this into the salad.

Lettuce or chicory leaves

Serve the salad in a nest of leaves. Also suitable for an hors d'oeuvre.

RICE SALAD

COOKING TIME: 15 mins: QUANTITIES for 4

4 oz rice (125 g): 2 tsp salt: ½ pt water (¼ l)

Bring to the boil, stir once, cover and reduce the heat to simmer until all the water is absorbed. Stir to fluff up.

3 Tbs French dressing

Dress the rice while it is still hot and then put aside to cool.

8 oz (250 g) cooked chicken or shellfish or a mixture of these with some hard-boiled egg, or a mixture of chicken, ham and egg: a little diced cucumber, tomato, sweet peppers, celery, raisins and green herbs

Mix in the chosen ingredients.

Lettuce leaves

Line the salad bowl with washed and dried leaves and pile the rice mixture in the centre.

CHAPTER SIXTEEN

Fruit is Indispensable

IT is perfect on its own to end a meal or to serve with the cheese, to serve for breakfast, to start a meal and to make simple puddings.

Home-grown fruits are supplemented by fresh, frozen and canned fruits from many countries while accelerated freeze-dried fruits are a future possibility. For tips on buying and storing fruit, see pages 26 and 34.

CANNED FRUITS

Keep a selection of these in a cool store cupboard. They have a storage life of 12 months or more.

The following varieties are generally available:

Apple sauce—to serve with pork, duck, lamb and other meats. Also use in the same way as apple purée.

Apple purée

Apple with Blackberries—can be used in pies and tarts; also use in apple crumble and fruit salads

Apricots

Bilberries

Blackcurrants

Cherries
Cranberries
Cumquats
Damsons
Fruit cocktail
Fruit salad
Cape goldenberries or Cape gooseberries
Gooseberries
Grapes
Grapefruit
Green figs
Green grapes
Grenadillas
Guavas
Lichees
Loganberries
Mandarins
Mangoes
Melon cubes
Paw-Paws
Peaches
Pears
Pineapple, cubes, pieces, rings, fingers, slices
Plums
Prunes
Raspberries
Rhubarb
Strawberries

FROZEN FRUITS

If you have a freezer, keep some of each of these in stock. They only take an hour or so to defrost and can be defrosted more quickly by turning them into a basin and standing this in warm water. Those frozen without sugar are the most useful as they can then have as much or as little added as you like or as the recipe requires. Use in the same way as fresh fruit.

Sliced apple
Blackberries
Blackcurrants
Blueberries
Gooseberries
Loganberries
Raspberries
Strawberries

FRUIT WITH CHEESE. Any raw fruit is pleasant with cheese but most people favour either apples, pears or grapes. If the fruit is to be eaten without peeling it should be washed and dried carefully. Serve the cheese on a board or cheese dish and the fruit in a bowl. The fruit takes the place of bread or biscuits so there is no need to serve these as well.

FRUIT SALAD. This can be purchased ready made in a number of forms. It is sold canned as fruit salad or fruit cocktail (the latter usually cut in smaller pieces), as citrus fruit salad (grapefruit and orange) or as tropical fruit salad (imported variety containing tropical fruits). A very good fruit salad can be made with a mixture of canned and fresh fruits, especially when some of the canned tropical fruits are used. Defrosted frozen fruits are also a welcome addition, especially raspberries. In summer time use ripe gooseberries, fresh raspberries and red currants in equal amounts. Fresh peaches and raspberries are delicious together.

SYRUP FOR FRUIT SALADS. This can be some of the juice from canned fruits with the addition of lemon or orange juice or some cider or liqueur. For fresh fruit salad make the following syrup:

QUANTITIES for 4

2–4 oz sugar or honey (4–8 Tbs or 60–120 g): ½ pt water or half cider or wine and half water (1 c or ¼ l)

Heat these together until the sugar and honey dissolve and then cool before using. If liquid honey is used the water need not be heated. Just stir for a minute or two. This is the quickest way of producing a syrup.

1 lb fruit (½ kg)

Fresh fruit can be cut in fairly small pieces but it is better to leave canned fruit in larger pieces otherwise the salad tends to look messy. Any salad can have a little Kirsch or other liqueur added for extra flavour and a few flaked almonds add contrast in texture.

FRUIT COMPÔTE OR STEWED FRUIT. The simplest way of cooking this is either in a casserole in the oven or in the top of a double boiler.

COOKING TIME: ½ hr upwards, depending on variety
TEMPERATURE E 325–350°, G 2–3

2–4 oz (60–120 g) sugar or honey per lb of fruit

Prepare the fruit according to the variety, slicing and cutting large fruits in pieces or quarters and leaving small ones whole. Put the fruit in a casserole or in the top of a double boiler. Add the sugar or honey and just enough water to moisten the bottom of the dish. For juicy fruits like berries and rhubarb no water will be needed. Quinces and hard fruits will need ½ pt water (1 c or ¼ l) per lb of fruit. Cover and cook slowly until the fruit is just tender, time depending on the variety, size and type of fruit.

FRUIT FOOL. Best fruits to use for this are apricots, black-currants, damsons, gooseberries, loganberries, mangoes, plums, prunes, raspberries, rhubarb or strawberries.

Use either raw, canned or stewed fruit and make the purée using the electric blender or a mechanical sieve (see page 157).

QUANTITIES for 4–6

½ pt thick raw or cooked fruit purée (1 c or ¼ l): lemon or orange rind or juice or spices to taste: sugar to taste

Sweeten and flavour the purée to taste and leave it to become quite cold. It must be very thick otherwise the fool will be runny. If canned fruit is used, drain it of syrup before making the fruit into a purée.

¼ pt evaporated milk (½ c or 1 ½ dl), or ½ pt whipping cream (1 c or ¼ l)

Whip the evaporated milk or cream until it is stiff. Fold in the fruit purée and ·put in individual serving dishes. Chill and garnish to taste.
Serve with a:

Crisp biscuit

FRUIT WITH YOGHURT. Suitable for raw or frozen berries.

QUANTITIES for 4

1 lb berries (½ kg): juice of 1 small lemon or 2 Tbs canned juice: ½ pt yoghurt (1 c or ¼ l) or 2 small jars: sugar to taste

Wash fresh berries and drain them thoroughly. Defrost frozen berries. Gently combine all the ingredients, sweetening to taste.
Serve in a bowl or in individual dishes.

FRUIT PURÉE OR PULP

QUANTITIES Allow 1 lb fruit (½ kg) for ½ pt purée (1 c or ¼ l)
(a little less if the purée is made in an electric blender)

If canned fruit is used to make a thick purée, it should be drained
from the syrup before sieving or pulping. In that case more than a
1 lb (½ kg) tin of fruit will be needed to make ½ pt (¼ l) purée
but this will depend on the relative amounts of fruit and syrup
which varies considerably with different brands of canned fruit.
Fruit for a purée may be raw, cooked, canned or frozen. For
cooked fruits, use the casserole method, see page 155. Raw fruits
should be soft-ripe and frozen ones defrosted. Apples have the best
flavour if baked in their skins and then the pulp scraped out. The
quickest way to make the purée is to put it in an electric blender.
Failing that, use a mechanical sieve or rub the fruit through a nylon
sieve, using a wooden spoon for rubbing.

FRUIT CRISP OR CRUMBLE

COOKING TIME: about 1 hr: QUANTITIES for 3–4
TEMPERATURE E 350°, G 3

1 lb fruit (½ kg): ¼ tsp cinnamon or other spice (optional): ⅛
pt water (¼ c or ¾ dl) (none for berries)

Peel or wash fresh fruit. Slice or cut apples and rhubarb in small
pieces. Drain canned fruit. Frozen berries need no defrosting. Put
the fruit in a pie-dish or other baking dish and add the spice and
water, using some of the liquid from canned fruit.

2 oz flour (6 Tbs or 60 g): 1 oz rolled oats (¼ c or 30 g): 2–4 oz
light brown sugar (¼–½ c or 60–120 g): 2 oz butter (4 Tbs or 60 g)

Mix the dry ingredients in a basin. Melt the butter and stir it into
the flour mixture until it makes a crumbly consistency. Sprinkle
this on top of the fruit and bake until the fruit is tender and the
top golden brown. Serve hot or cold with:

Cream or custard

ALTERNATIVE TOPPING Use 4 oz (or 120 g) ready-mix short crust mix,
packet or home made. Add 2 oz (60 g) sugar to it and sprinkle on
top of the fruit.

FRUIT MOUSSE

QUANTITIES for 4

½ pt very thick fruit purée sweetened to taste (1 c or ¼ l): 2 eggs

Separate the whites and yolks of the eggs and heat the purée with the yolks, stirring until it thickens but not boils. Beat the whites until stiff enough to stand up in peaks and fold into the fruit mixture. Pour into individual dishes, cool and then chill. Garnish to taste.

APPLES. Serve raw ones plain as dessert or with nuts or cheese; also sliced thinly in fruit salad.

Use cooking apples: to make Fruit Fool, see page 156; Fruit Crisp, see page 157; Pies, see page 199; Fruit Mousse, see page 158; and for baking and making Apple Purée, see page 159. Canned apple sauce and purée, use as freshly made purée.

BAKED APPLES

COOKING TIME: 40–45 mins: QUANTITIES one apple per person: TEMPERATURE E 400°, G6

Large and perfect cooking apples: ⅛ oz butter per apple (¼ Tbs or 4 g): dates, raisins, nuts, chopped peel and some spices for stuffing (optional): 1 Tbs sugar, honey, syrup or black treacle per apple: water or cider to come half-way up the baking dish

Wash the apples. If they are to be stuffed, remove cores using an apple corer. Slit the skins in a ring about half-way up the sides of the apple. This prevents bursting during cooking. Place the apples in a shallow baking dish (not tin) and fill the centres for stuffed ones. Put the butter and sweetening on top. Pour in the liquid and bake until they feel tender when pierced with a cooking fork. It is an improvement to baste them once or twice during cooking.

Serve hot or cold.

BAKED APPLES WITH RUM. Stuff the apples with apricot jam and sprinkle with flaked almonds or nibs. Use brown sugar for the sweetening and for the liquid, half rum and half water. Baste with the liquid during cooking and serve hot.

APPLE SAUCE OR PURÉE. Wash the apples and cut them up roughly. Cook with only enough water to prevent burning. Then rub through a sieve and add sugar to taste. It takes less time to do this than to peel and core the apples before cooking. If frozen apples are used, they can be cooked with the sugar and then mashed to a pulp or put in the electric blender to make a smooth purée.

Suggestions for using apple purée or pulp

1. Two-thirds fill individual glass dishes with sweetened apple purée or pulp. This can be flavoured to taste with a little grated orange or lemon rind or with some ground ginger or spices. Cover the top with a layer of whipped cream, flavoured with rum or liqueur to taste. Top with grated chocolate or chocolate vermicelli or similarly prepared chocolate and garnish with cherry or fruit. Serve chilled.

2. Sweeten apple purée to taste and, when cold, add 2 Tbs rum per portion. Put in individual serving dishes. Peel and slice one orange for each two portions and decorate the purée with this or use canned mandarins. Garnish with red fruit or glacé cherries. Just before serving sprinkle with caster sugar. Serve cream separately.

3. Make Apple Fool, see page 156.

4. Make Apple Mousse, see page 158.

5. Sweeten the purée to taste and flavour with ground cinnamon. Serve cold in individual dishes and hand thin cream and crisp biscuits separately.

APPLE CHEESE CRUMBLE (a change from ordinary apple crumble and no more trouble).

COOKING TIME: 40–50 mins: QUANTITIES for 4
TEMPERATURE E 375°, G 5

1 *lb cooking apples* (½ *kg*): 2 *oz grated cheddar cheese* (½ *c or 60 g*)

Peel and slice the apples or use ready prepared frozen ones (¾–1 lb or 375–500 g). Buy the cheese ready grated if possible, from dairy or delicatessen. Mix apples and cheese in a baking or pie dish.

> *3 oz plain flour (½ c or 100 g): ½ tsp cinnamon: 3 oz brown sugar (6 Tbs or 100 g): pinch grated nutmeg*

Mix in a bowl.

> *2 oz butter or margarine (4 Tbs or 60 g)*

Have this softened and mix into the flour with the electric mixer as for short pastry. Alternatively, use 5 oz (150 g) ready mix short pastry, dry mix and add the other ingredients (sugar and spices). Sprinkle over the apples and bake until the fruit is tender. Serve hot or warm.

APRICOTS. If fresh apricots are really ripe and of good quality, serve them as dessert, otherwise stew them, cracking a few of the stones to extract the kernels which impart a pleasant flavour when they are cooked with the fruit. Canned apricots are served as a stewed fruit or with milk puddings, as Fruit Flans, see page 193, Fruit Fool, see page 156, Ice-cream, see page 188 or Fruit Mousse, see page 158.

BANANAS. Raw bananas are served with breakfast cereal or in fruit salads or just plain for dessert. They are also baked, see page 160, fried, see page 161, grilled, see page 161. Other recipes, see pages 162–3. Dried bananas are eaten as a sweetmeat or in place of other dried fruit in cooking.

Banana flakes are served as a breakfast cereal.

BAKED BANANAS

COOKING TIME: 20 mins: QUANTITIES Allow 1 banana per person: TEMPERATURE E 375°, G 5

Method 1
Wash and dry the bananas. Place in a baking dish and cook until the

skins burst. Peel off a strip of skin, sprinkle the banana with salt and pepper and serve as a vegetable with grilled lamb chops or beef steak.

Method 2

Skin the bananas and place them in a shallow fireproof dish. Sprinkle them with sugar and lemon juice and dot with butter. Bake until they are speckled with brown. Serve hot or cold, with cream.

A little rum may be added towards the end of cooking. Set light to the rum just before serving.

Method 3

Skin the bananas and cut them in quarters lengthwise. Place them in a shallow baking dish and sprinkle with lemon juice and finely grated lemon rind. Cover them with a layer of stoned, cooked or canned prunes or red plums. Pour in enough of the juice from the fruit to barely cover the bananas. Bake until the bananas are tender. Serve warm or chilled with or without cream.

FRIED BANANAS. If the bananas are large ones, peel and halve them lengthwise and then crosswise. If they are small, simply halve them lengthwise. Dredge them with seasoned flour and fry in shallow fat, oil or butter until they are tender and soft. Use a fish slice or similar tool to lift them out of the pan.

If they are to accompany a savoury dish, sprinkle them with lemon juice, e.g. for serving with pork, bacon, beef or poultry.

If they are to be served for a sweet course, serve with jam, Melba sauce, custard or milk pudding.

To serve with bacon for breakfast, fry the bacon first and then the bananas in the bacon fat.

GRILLED BANANAS. Peel the bananas and brush them with melted butter or with oil. Sprinkle with salt and grill under a moderate heat until they are tender, about 8 mins. Turn once during cooking.

Serve with other grilled food or as a garnish to any savoury dish, or with grilled bacon for breakfast, or as part of a Kebab.

F

BANANA MOULD

QUANTITIES for 4

2 ripe bananas: 1 Tbs sugar: 1 Tbs gelatine dissolved in 4 Tbs hot water: ½ pt single cream (1 c or ¼ l)

Put all ingredients into the electric blender and mix until smooth. Pour into individual glass dishes or moulds and leave to set. Garnish with:

Whipped cream, jam or fruit

BANANA AND GRAPEFRUIT COCKTAIL

QUANTITIES for 4–6

4 small bananas: 1 lb can grapefruit segments (½ kg): 2 oranges

Peel and slice the bananas. Drain the grapefruit. Add fruit to the bananas. Squeeze the oranges and pour the juice over the grapefruit and bananas with enough of the grapefruit juice just to cover. Chill.

Maraschino cherries

Serve garnished with cherries.

BANANA AND CHOCOLATE CREAM

QUANTITIES for 4

4 bananas: 1 oz caster sugar (2 Tbs or 30 g): ¼ pt double cream (½ c or 1 ½ dl): vanilla essence

Skin the bananas and mash them with a fork. Add the sugar and vanilla to taste and then the cream.

Juice of 1 lemon or 2 Tbs canned juice or 1–2 Tbs rum

Add to the bananas and put the mixture in four individual dishes.

2 oz (60 g) chocolate vermicelli or grated chocolate: Glacé cherries

Cover the top of the mixture with the chocolate and decorate with a cherry. Serve cold.

FRESH RED CURRANTS WITH BANANA SAUCE

QUANTITIES for 4

1 lb red currants (½ kg)

Wash, remove stalks and put the fruit in individual dishes.

4 ripe bananas: juice of 1 lemon or 2 Tbs canned juice, 3 oz caster sugar (6 Tbs or 100 g): ½ pt single cream (1 c or ¼ l)

Put these in the electric blender and mix until a smooth sauce is formed. Pour it over the currants.

BILBERRIES OR BLUE BERRIES. Used in pies or to make fruit compôte.

BLACKBERRIES. Use fresh or frozen ones to make Fruit Crisp, see page 157; for Fruit with Yoghurt, see page 156; for Fruit Mousse, see page 158 and Fruit Fool, see page 156. Also to make pies (with apple) and tarts. Canned blackberries—use as stewed fruit or drained to make a purée for fool and mousse.

CHERRIES. Fresh dessert cherries are best served raw in place of a pudding or as dessert, or in fruit salad (but stone first). Cooking cherries are used to make compôte, flans and tarts or pies. Frozen ones: use as fresh. Canned ones: as compôte or in fruit salad.

CRANBERRIES. Available as raw, or canned sauce. They are only suitable for cooking and need plenty of sugar. Use for Cranberry Sauce, page 60 (Gooseberry Sauce) or to make Fruit Tart, see page 200 or Upside-down Cake, see page 214.

DAMSONS. See Plums, page 169.

CAPE GOLDENBERRIES OR GOOSEBERRIES. Available canned. Serve as stewed fruit or in a fruit salad or to make a flan, see page 197.

GOOSEBERRIES. Ripe ones serve as dessert or in fruit salad. Green and frozen ones: use to make Fruit Compôte, see page 155, Fruit Fool, see page 156, Fruit Crisp, see page 157, Fruit Mousse, see page 158, or Fruit pies or tarts, see page 200 or Fruit Flan, see page 197.

Canned gooseberries are served as stewed fruit, added to fruit salads or used to make a purée for fruit fool and mousse.

To prepare fresh gooseberries wash and top and tail using scissors.

GRAPES. Wash and serve as dessert or with cheese or in fruit salad. Canned ones are used as stewed fruit or in fruit salad or to make a flan, see page 197.

GRAPEFRUIT. Fresh grapefruit is served as a breakfast fruit, for hors d'oeuvre, for fruit cocktails, to add to fruit and savoury salads. Canned grapefruit juice is used as a beverage or to add to fruit salads and as the liquid for making jellies.

PREPARING FRESH GRAPEFRUIT

Segments Cut off all peel and pith exposing the flesh. Hold the fruit over a plate to catch the juice, and with a small saw-edged knife, cut along the sides of each segment to loosen it from the membrane on each side. When all segments have been removed, squeeze the membrane to extract all remaining juice. For serving at breakfast, sprinkle with a little caster sugar or liquid honey. To serve as a fruit cocktail, sprinkle with a little caster sugar and some kirsch or maraschino. Garnish with a maraschino cherry.

Serving in the Skin Cut the fruit in half at right angles to the stem end. Remove pips. Using a small sharp, serrated knife cut along the side of each segment to loosen it from the membrane. Then cut round the edges and down underneath with a grapefruit knife until all is loosened. Core and membrane should then lift out in one piece leaving the segments in position. Garnish the centre with a cherry and sprinkle with sugar or liquid honey or serve plain.

GREENGAGES. See Plums page 169.

GRENADILLAS OR PASSION FRUIT. Only the pulp is used, added to fruit salad or to make fruit drinks; also added to whipped cream as a cake filling. Canned grenadilla is used in the same way.

GRENADILLA WHIP

QUANTITIES for 4

½ *pt double cream* (1 *c or 6 l*)

Whip until stiff and then fold in.

8 *oz canned grenadilla* (2 *small tins or 250 g*)

Pile in serving dishes and chill.

GUAVAS. Usually only available canned or as guava juice or jelly. Use the canned fruit alone or to add to fruit salad.

KUMQUAT. Occasionally available raw and may be cooked or eaten raw. Also sold as a very sweet pickle in cans.

LOGANBERRIES. For dessert raw ones need to be very ripe. They are more usually cooked as are frozen ones. Used as a Fruit Compôte, see page 155, or to make a Fruit Fool, see page 156, or Mousse, see page 158, or for Fruit Tart, see page 200, or Fruit Crisp, see page 157.

LEMONS. Available fresh or as canned and bottled juice. Used mainly for flavouring and giving zest to other fruit mixtures, e.g. fruit salad.

LICHEES. When available fresh, the brown skin is peeled off and the white pulp eaten either alone or added to fruit salad. Canned ones are used plain or to add to salads. They have a delicate flavour so be careful with the choice of the other fruits in the salad.

MANDARINS (used as oranges, see page 167).
Canned mandarins are very useful for many dishes, especially where the appearance of the fruit is important. The segments are firm and perfect.

MANGO. Usually only available canned or as chutney. The canned fruit is excellent by itself or in a fruit salad or to make a Fruit Fool, see page 156.

MELON. To prepare melon, wash the skin and then cut the fruit in slices. Remove the seeds. It can then be served plain or with caster sugar and/or ground ginger handed separately.
Other ways of serving are:
1. Cantaloup melon with ice-cream.
2. Diced melon either alone as a fruit cocktail or with other fruits, dressed with syrup or fruit juice and a little liqueur.
3. Small melons cut in half, the seeds removed and the centres filled with port wine. Leave to stand for some time before serving.
4. Serve diced melon in a heavy syrup with a little brandy or liqueur and some raw red currants or raspberries.
5. Serve melon cubes with some raw blackberries and whipped cream or single cream.
6. Dress melon cubes with equal quantities of lemon and orange juice and enough rosehip syrup to sweeten to taste.

PLUM AND MELON SALAD

QUANTITIES for 4

1 lb ripe plums (½ kg): ½ small melon: 6 oz orange juice (12 Tbs or 2 dl): 1 oz honey (1 Tbs or 30 g) or to taste

Wash and stone the plums and cut them in small pieces. Peel and dice the melon. Mix the two fruits and add the orange juice mixed with the honey. Chill before serving.

NECTARINE. Serve raw for dessert or in fruit salads or use to make a Fruit Compôte, see page 155.

ORANGES. Best served raw as a dessert fruit or as a raw fruit salad. Large ones are sometimes prepared and served as grapefruit, see page 164. The juice is available dried, frozen or canned and is used for beverages and for adding to fruit salads and for flavouring. Canned orange and grapefruit segments and canned mandarins are all useful varieties.

PAW-PAW. Available canned and used plain or in fruit salads.

PEACHES. Raw, ripe ones are eaten for dessert or added to fruit salads or served with ice-cream and Melba sauce. Canned ones are served as fruit compôte or added to fruit salad or served with grilled meat or ham.

SPICED PEACHES

COOKING TIME: 15–20 mins: QUANTITIES for 4–6

2 lb can peach halves (1 kg)

Drain the peaches and put the syrup in a small pan.

¼ pt water (½ c or 1½ dl): 2 in (5 cm) stick cinnamon: 6 cloves: pinch of ground ginger

Add these to the syrup, bring to the boil and simmer for 15–20 mins. Strain onto the peaches and chill before serving.
Serve plain with:

Cream

PEARS. Raw, ripe ones are served as dessert or to make fruit salad or with ice-cream and chocolate sauce. They can also be fried in butter and served with chocolate sauce or baked in the oven. Raw cooking ones are stewed, see page 155. They are particularly good served with rice, see page 178 and with preserved ginger for flavouring, see over:

GINGER PEARS

QUANTITIES for 4

4 ripe pears

Peel, core and slice. Arrange in individual dishes.

2 large oranges: 1 lemon: 1 oz castor sugar (2 Tbs or 30 g)

Squeeze the fruit and combine the juices with the sugar. Stir until sugar dissolves. Pour it over the pears.

Chopped preserved ginger

Add ginger to taste and chill the fruit before serving.

PINEAPPLE. Fresh ones are sliced, skin and cores removed, and served as dessert, preferably with a little kirsch poured over and a little sugar sprinkled on.

Canned pineapple is used plain or added to fruit salads. Pineapple rings are grilled or fried to serve with meat. Use also to make Upside-down cake, see page 214. Canned pineapple juice is used to add to other beverages, or on its own to make jellies and other cold sweets. The juice makes a pleasant cold sweet if it is used in place of milk to make a custard.

PINEAPPLE ST. REMO

QUANTITIES for 4

4 rings canned pineapple: ½ pt lemon jelly (¼ l) using some of the canned pineapple juice in place of water

Arrange the pineapple on a serving dish. Pour the jelly over it just to cover the fruit. Leave to set. At this stage it may be stored in the refrigerator and then finished just before serving.

2 medium oranges: coarse white sugar

Peel the oranges thickly, removing all pith. Cut each in half and remove any pips and central core or pith. Place cut side down on the slices of pineapple. Put a heap of sugar on top of each and serve with:

Cream

PLUMS. Ripe ones are used as dessert or to make fruit salads or Fruit Flans, see page 197. Cooked and canned ones are used for fruit compôte, to make Fruit Fool, see page 156, or Fruit Mousse, see page 158.

POMEGRANATES. The pulp is added to fruit salads or fruit cocktails.

PRUNES Cooked or canned prunes are used as stewed fruit or to make Fruit Fool, see page 156, or Fruit Mousse, see page 158. Prune juice is available canned to use as a beverage either alone or mixed with other fruit juices. It is also added to fruit cocktails or fruit salads.

PRUNES IN CIDER

COOKING TIME: 35 mins: QUANTITIES for 4

8 *oz prunes:* ½ *pt water* (1 *c or* ¼ *l*)

Soak these together overnight or until the prunes are plump. Drain, keeping the water.

2 *oz sugar* (4 *Tbs or* 60 *g*)

Add to the prune water and boil until syrupy. Add the prunes.

3 *pieces preserved ginger:* ⅛ *pt cider* (¼ *c or* ¾ *dl*)

Chop the ginger and add it and the cider to the prunes. Simmer for ½ hr or until the prunes are tender. Serve cold with:

Cream

QUICK METHOD OF PREPARING PRUNES. Use plump prunes and no cooking will be needed. For each pound of prunes allow 1 quart (4 c or 1 l) boiling water. Pour this over the prunes, cool, and leave them to soak for 24 hrs or longer in the refrigerator. Add sugar to taste and a little grated orange or lemon rind.

QUINCES. Sometimes available in the late autumn. Usually peeled, cored, sliced and stewed, see page 155. Very good served with rice mould, see page 176. Powdered cinnamon blends well with the flavour.

RASPBERRIES. The best way of using fresh or frozen ones is raw with sugar and cream. Raw or canned they are used to make Fruit with Yoghurt, see page 156, Fruit Fool, see page 156, Fruit Mousse, see page 158 and Fruit Tarts, see page 200.

RHUBARB. Fresh rhubarb is used for pies and tarts, see page 200, or to make Crisp, see page 157, or to make a compôte, see page 155.

Canned rhubarb is served as stewed fruit or the drained fruit is used to make a purée for Fruit Mousse and Fruit Fool.

BAKED SPICED RHUBARB

COOKING TIME: 25 mins: TEMPERATURE E 400°, G 6
QUANTITIES for 4–6

2 lb rhubarb (1 kg)

Cut off the tops of the sticks and trim the root ends. Wash rhubarb well and cut it in 1 inch pieces. Put in a casserole.

6–8 oz sugar (¾–1 c or 180–250 g): 1 inch (2½ cm) stick of cinnamon or a little grated cinnamon: 4 cloves

Sprinkle sugar over rhubarb and add spices. Cover and bake until tender but not mushy. Leave it covered while cooling, and serve cold.

STRAWBERRIES. Raw or frozen ones are best served with cream and sugar, but can be used for Fruit Fool, see page 156, Fruit Mousse, see page 158, or Fruit Flan, see page 197. Canned ones are added to fruit salad or drained and the purée used to make Mousse or Fruit Fool.

CHAPTER SEVENTEEN

Useful Rice

ALWAYS keep some rice in the store-cupboard. It requires no preparation and it can be cooked quickly for savoury dishes and to serve in place of potatoes, or it can be left to cook very slowly in the oven to make puddings. Ready-cooked rice is also available and only needs heating.

There are some dehydrated meals including rice, for example, Paella, and curry with rice, while canned varieties include creamed rice pudding, cooked rice, curried meats and chicken or prawns with rice.

Different varieties of rice are used for different kinds of cooking. These include:

Rounded Grain, of short or medium length, used for puddings. Carolina rice is a well-known variety of this type. In countries where Risotto, Paella and Pilaf are national dishes, a special type of round rice is used which does not have a tendency to become sticky as pudding rice does.

Long Grain, of which Patna is the best known variety. Provided the rice is not overcooked, the long thin grains will remain separate. It is the variety preferred for boiled rice and some people prefer a long grain for Risotto and similar dishes.

Par-boiled Rice is partly cooked under steam pressure before milling. This type of rice contains more minerals and vitamins than ordinary milled rice. It also absorbs more water during cooking and remains separate and fluffy. It is sold in packets complete with cooking directions.

Pre-cooked or Quick Cooking Rice is sold almost completely cooked and only requires to he re-heated. This too is sold in packets with cooking directions.

Brown Rice has only some of the branny layers removed during milling and contains more vitamins and minerals than white rice. It has more flavour, takes longer to cook and absorbs more water.

Ground Rice is coarsely milled white rice used for making puddings, for thickening soups and in making cakes and biscuits.

Flaked Rice is used for making puddings.

Breakfast Cereal is made from white rice, the most well known being puffed rice.

BOILED RICE. Where directions are given on the packets it is advisable to follow these as the rice is often processed and needs special cooking methods. The following methods are for ordinary long grain rice. Round grain rice may also be boiled by these methods but most of it tends to clump together instead of the grains remaining separate.

COOKING TIME: 15–20 mins: QUANTITIES for 4

8 oz rice (1 c or 250 g): 1 pt water (2 c or ½ l): 1 tsp salt

Put all in a pan and bring to the boil, stir once, put on the lid. Reduce the heat and simmer for 15 mins without stirring or lifting the lid. If convenient, this part of the cooking can be done in a moderate oven. After 15 mins test a few grains by squeezing them between thumb and finger and if there is no hard core of un-cooked starch, the rice is done. By this time all the water should be absorbed. To produce a dry rice, fluff it with a fork, cover and stand it in a warm place for 5–10 minutes to steam dry but do not have enough heat to continue cooking the rice. Turn into a hot dish and fluff lightly with a fork.

COOKING IN A CASSEROLE. Use the above proportions. Put rice and salt in the casserole and add boiling water. Cover and cook in a moderate oven (E 350°, G 4) for about 40 mins. Test as before and, if necessary, remove the lid of the casserole for a few minutes at the end of cooking to allow the last water to evaporate. Fluff lightly with a fork.

RE-HEATING BOILED RICE. Cold boiled rice keeps well in a tightly covered dish in the refrigerator for up to a week, or in the larder for 2–3 days.

To re-heat it, put the rice in a covered saucepan with a few tablespoons of water and stand the pan over a low heat. Shake the pan occasionally and in a few moments the rice will be hot and fluffy and ready to serve.

FRIED RICE. Fry a little finely chopped onion in butter or oil until it is soft and beginning to brown. Add dry cooked rice from store and stir and heat until all the fat is absorbed and the rice is beginning to brown. Add chopped green herbs and season to taste. Serve with meat or fish.

OPTIONAL ADDITIONS
Chopped canned pineapple and chopped salted almonds.
Raisins and chopped almonds.
Fry some chopped green pepper with the onion.
Chopped celery and mushrooms fried with the onion.
Chopped tomato.

SERVING RICE. It is usually served in a bowl or vegetable dish for people to help themselves. Or it may be heaped in a ring round the edges of a flat serving dish or shallow entrée dish and the meat or other accompaniment put in the centre. This enables the sauce to mix with the rice. Use this method of service for individual portions too.

KEDGEREE (a good dish for advance preparation).

COOKING TIME: 20 mins from raw ingredients: 5 mins from pre-prepared: QUANTITIES for 4

4 c ready boiled rice (8 oz or 250 g raw): 1 lb (½ kg) cooked fish, use fillets, e.g. boil-in-the-bag frozen kipper or frozen smoked fish, 2 hard-boiled eggs

These can be prepared and stored in the refrigerator until the meal is to be served. Then flake the fish. Separate whites and yolks of the eggs and rub yolks through a sieve. Chop whites coarsely.

2 oz butter or margarine (4 Tbs or 60 g): pinch of ground nutmeg: salt and pepper

Melt the fat in a large pan and add the fish and rice. Cook over a gentle heat until all is hot. Add the seasonings and egg whites and heat again. Pile on a hot dish and decorate with the egg yolk. Garnish with:

Parsley and wedges of lemon

RICE SALAD. See Salads, page 152.

RISOTTO

COOKING TIME: 25–30 mins: QUANTITIES for 4–6

4 oz fat or oil (½ c or 120 g): 6 oz onions (180 g)

Skin and chop the onion or put it through a mechanical chopper or mincer. Heat the fat or oil in a heavy frying pan or sauté pan (about 9–10 in or 23–25 cm diameter). Fry the onion in the fat until it begins to brown.

12 oz rice (1½ c or 375 g)

Add the raw rice and cook for a few moments longer, stirring all the time.

2 pt stock (4 c or 1 l) or use chicken cubes and water

Add about a quarter of the stock to the rice and cook gently for 15–20 mins adding the rest of the stock gradually. By the time the rice is tender all the stock should be absorbed.

4 oz (120 g) mushrooms, kidneys or other meat (use cooked or canned): salt and pepper

Cut the mushrooms or meat in small pieces and add to the rice just before serving. Season to taste.

Grated cheese

Hand this separately to be sprinkled on at table. Serve the risotto in individual dishes or piled up on a large platter.

LIVER PILAF

COOKING TIME: ¾ hr: QUANTITIES for 4–6

2 oz butter (4 Tbs or 60 g): 1 pt chicken stock or chicken cubes and water (2 c or ½ l)

Put in a large pan and bring to the boil.

8 oz long grain rice (1 c or 250 g)

Add to the stock, stir and then cook very slowly. This can be done in a slow oven (E 350°, G 3). Cook until the rice is quite tender, 20–30 mins, and the stock all absorbed.

Salt and pepper

Season the rice to taste. Dish in a mound on a hot plate or pack into a border mould or individual moulds. Keep hot.

8–12 oz liver (250–375 g): 1–2 oz butter (2–4 Tbs or 30–60 g): salt and pepper

Cut the liver in small cubes. Heat the butter and fry the liver in it until it is lightly browned. Season with salt and pepper. Pile this on top of the rice.

If liked, garnish with:

Green peas or baked or grilled tomatoes

RICE PUDDINGS. There are many makes of canned rice pudding which is usually a creamy and palatable product and a most useful article for the store-cupboard. If you sometimes want a change from the standardised flavour and texture of these, to make your own rice pudding is not a time-consuming job. The cooking time is long if you want a creamy result but the preparation of the ingredients is only a matter of a couple of minutes and the oven will look after the rest.

Two recipes are given below, one for traditional Baked Rice Pudding and the other for making a Rice Mould, though this latter mixture can be used for a variety of cold sweets based on rice. The other recipes are suitable for use with the Rice Mould mixture or with canned rice pudding.

BAKED RICE PUDDING

COOKING TIME: 2–3 hrs: TEMPERATURE E 300°, G 1:
QUANTITIES for 3–4

1 ½ oz rice (3 Tbs or 45 g): ½ oz sugar (1 Tbs or 15 g): *strip of fresh orange or lemon rind (optional): grated nutmeg (optional) pinch of salt: 1 pt milk (2 c or ½ l)*

Put all the ingredients except the nutmeg in a pie dish or other baking dish. Sprinkle nutmeg on top according to taste. Bake as slowly as possible because the long slow cooking produces a creamy pudding. Neither temperature nor time are critical and the baking can fit in with other foods. If you are at hand during cooking, to stir in the top skin once or twice during the first hour of cooking helps to make it creamy. The last part of the cooking should be undisturbed to allow a skin to form on top.

RICE MOULD

COOKING TIME: 2–4 hrs: QUANTITIES for 4
TEMPERATURE E 250–325°, G ¼–4

2 oz pudding rice (4 Tbs or 60 g): 2–3 *thin strips lemon rind:* 1 ½ oz sugar (3 Tbs or 45 g): *pinch of salt:* ½ oz butter (1 Tbs or 15 g): 1 pt milk (2 c or ½ l)

Put all in a covered casserole and cook gently. If the temperature is kept low this will not boil over and does not form a skin. Remove from the oven and stir in:

1 *egg, beaten*

Pour the pudding into a greased mould and leave to become cold. The cooked pudding will keep well in the refrigerator to be used at a later meal.

GINGER RICE

Rice mould recipe or a 1 lb can of rice pudding (½ kg): chopped preserved ginger in syrup: some of the ginger syrup: glacé cherries and angelica

Mix in chopped ginger to taste and a little of the syrup. Pile the pudding in individual dishes and pour a little more syrup round the edge.

Garnish with cherry and angelica.

APRICOT RICE

Rice mould recipe or a 1 lb can of rice pudding (½ kg): 1 lb canned apricot halves (½ kg): split almonds: almond essence: angelica

Mound the rice in a serving dish or in individual dishes.

Drain the apricots and arrange in a pattern round the rice, or on top. Boil the juice until thick and syrupy, cool a little and add a few drops of almond essence. Brush this over the fruit. Decorate with the split almonds and angelica.

PINEAPPLE RICE

Rice mould recipe or a 1 lb can of rice pudding (½ kg): 1 lb tin pineapple rings (½ kg): maraschino cherries

Drain the pineapple. Mound the rice and arrange the pineapple rings in a circle round the base. Section one ring and put on top of the mound. Put a maraschino cherry in the centre of each piece of pineapple.

CHOCOLATE RICE (using Rice Mould recipe).
Omit the lemon rind from the basic pudding mixture.

  1 oz cocoa powder (3 Tbs or 20 g)

Mix cocoa with the sugar and a little milk and add to the other
ingredients. Finish as before. Unmould and serve with either:

  Canned or stewed pears or canned mandarin oranges

RAISIN RICE PUDDING (using canned rice pudding)

COOKING TIME: 2–3 mins: QUANTITIES for 3–4

  1 lb can rice pudding (½ kg): 2 oz seeded raisins (⅓ c or 60 g):
  2 Tbs double cream: ½ tsp vanilla essence

Mix these together and put into a fireproof dish.

  1 ½–2 oz fine brown sugar (3–4 Tbs or 45–60 g)

Sprinkle over the top of the pudding and put under the grill until
the sugar melts. Cool and then chill. If the pudding is chilled for
some time, the brown sugar will mix in with the rest and give a
caramel colour and an excellent flavour.

ALTERNATIVE Heat the pudding mixture and add an egg to it before
adding the raisins and vanilla. After the sugar has been melted,
this pudding can be served hot.

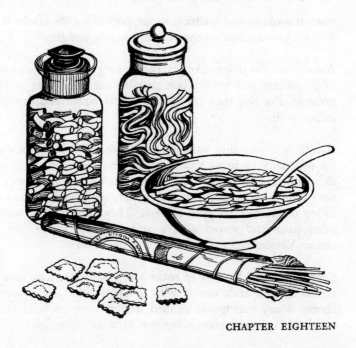

CHAPTER EIGHTEEN

All Pasta Cook Quickly

THE two pasta most widely used in Britain are macaroni and spaghetti, which are available canned as well as raw. Pasta are all very useful because they need no preparation, the cooking required is very little and they can be served in a variety of ways. Pasta can also take the place of potatoes in a main meal, though their nutritive value is somewhat different.

There are about 150 different shapes of pasta made but not all of them are sold in the average shop. Those most readily available are:

Canneloni which is a large flat pasta, usually stuffed like a pancake. They are available canned and make a good snack meal or can be served as a first course in a main meal.

Macaroni is sold either in long sticks or cut in short pieces. Some of the packet macaroni has been specially treated for quicker than normal cooking and instructions are printed on the labels. It is also sold as canned macaroni cheese and macaroni pudding.

Noodles are flat ribbon-like pasta containing egg. They are sold loose or in packets and are the best pasta to use with meat in place of potatoes. For this they are usually simply boiled and dressed with butter or oil.

Ravioli is a very thin pasta which is not dried but is made fresh for sale daily by firms specialising in its production. It is sold by delicatessens and Italian grocers. Ravioli consists of a paste rolled very thinly, cut in small squares which are joined in pairs with a filling of meat or chopped spinach. They are boiled in water like other pasta and served with a sauce or with butter and grated cheese. Various types of ravioli are available in cans.

Spaghetti is sold loose or in packets and usually as long sticks. It is served as a separate course with a sauce, either meat, tomato or cheese. Many varieties of canned spaghetti are on sale, including spaghetti in tomato sauce, Bolognese, Milanese, Romana.

Vermicelli consists of very fine sticks which are sold loose or in bundles tied in a loose knot. It is used chiefly for garnishing soup but also in the same way as spaghetti. Available plain, or as egg vermicelli.

Pasta for Garnishing Many fancy-shaped tiny pasta are made for garnishing soups, other larger shapes are used in the same way as macaroni and spaghetti. These shapes include alphabets, bows, rings, shells, stars, wheels and curled macaroni.

BOILING PASTA. Most of the varieties sold in packets contain cooking instructions. It is advisable to follow these as many pasta have been specially prepared for quick cooking and the traditional method may over-cook them. If there are no instructions use the following method:

COOKING TIME: 5–15 mins depending on the variety. 20 mins for ravioli:

QUANTITIES Allow 4 oz or more per person for a main dish (120 g)
2 oz if served with other things (60 g)

*For each pound of pasta allow 6–8 pt (3–4 l) water, 1 Tbs salt,
and 1 Tbs oil*

Bring the water to the boil and add oil and salt. The oil is not
essential but it enables the water to be kept from boiling over even
when the lid is kept on the pan, always provided the heat is not
left full on. Add the pasta gradually, keeping the water boiling all
the time. If it is a long pasta, put in one end letting the top pro-
trude above the pan and as the pasta softens it will curl down in
the water. Boil rapidly until it is just tender. It should still be firm or
have 'bite'. If cooked beyond this stage it becomes soft and clumps
together in a sticky mess. Drain well in a sieve or colander. Toss it
in a little olive oil to give it a shine, or use butter instead. The
simplest way of serving any pasta is with plenty of grated Parmesan
cheese or with a tomato sauce which is available in packet form or
use quick tomato sauce, see page 62.

WAYS OF SERVING CANNED MACARONI CHEESE

1. *To a 1 lb can (½ kg) of macaroni cheese add 2 oz (60 g)
chopped cooked ham.* Either heat through and brown in the oven
or heat in a pan and put in a dish to brown under the grill. Serve
with *tomato salad*.
2. Heat the macaroni cheese and serve it in place of potatoes with
veal or chicken.
3. Mix canned macaroni cheese with some canned tomatoes and a
little Worcester sauce. Bake in a moderate oven until heated
through, about 20 mins.

SPAGHETTI BOLOGNESE. This is sold canned. Canned
Bolognese sauce is available for adding to freshly cooked spaghetti
or use canned minced meat for the sauce as below:

COOKING TIME: 10 mins: QUANTITIES for 4

½–1 lb spaghetti (250–500 g): oil or butter

Boil the spaghetti in plenty of salted water until it is only just tender. Drain and toss in a little oil or butter and pile on a serving dish.

12–15 oz can minced beef steak (375–450 g) 1 Tbs tomato paste

Some minced beef already contains tomato, in which case omit the paste. Heat the mince and tomato while the spaghetti is cooking and then pour it into the centre of the cooked spaghetti.

Grated Parmesan cheese

Sprinkle thickly on top of the meat and serve at once.

BAKED SPAGHETTI AND EGG

COOKING TIME: 20 mins: TEMPERATURE E 400°, G 6
QUANTITIES for 4

1 lb can spaghetti in tomato sauce (½ kg)

Put in a shallow baking dish in the oven until the spaghetti is hot.

4 eggs: grated cheese

Make four small depressions in the spaghetti and slide an egg into each. Sprinkle the tops with grated cheese and return to the oven until the egg is lightly set and the cheese melted. Serve at once, garnished with:

Cress

NOODLES WITH SOUR CREAM

COOKING TIME: 10 mins: QUANTITIES for 4

8 oz cooked ham (250 g)

Buy this in slices and then cut the pile of slices lengthwise in strips and then crosswise to give small pieces.

1 lb noodles (½ kg)

Boil according to directions on the packet or see page 180. Drain.

2 oz butter (4 Tbs or 60 g)

Melt in the pan, add the noodles and ham and mix well.

½ pt cultured sour cream (2 small cartons or ¼ l): salt and pepper

Add to the noodles and mix well, making sure it is hot.

Grated Parmesan cheese

Serve the noodles on a hot dish and hand the cheese separately.

CHAPTER NINETEEN

For Those with a Sweet Tooth

THERE are plenty of ready-prepared puddings to choose from.

Varieties of canned puddings include:

Steamed sponge puddings of many flavours, some made with butter.
Apple dumplings.
Creamed milk puddings such as semolina, sago, rice, macaroni and tapioca.

Varieties of packet puddings include:

Instant desserts of many flavours.
Dessert powders.
Blancmange powders of many flavours.
Jellies and table creams.
Pudding mixes such as steamed sponge, bakewell, suet pudding, sponge flan, pancakes and batter pudding.
Ready mix ice-cream powder.

Varieties of frozen puddings include:
Mousses, chocolate, lemon, strawberry and raspberry.
Vanilla and many other ice-creams.

Many of the ready-prepared puddings simply need to be heated for serving while others have to be prepared in some way. Many can be used as a basis for quick puddings using additional ingredients to give an individual touch.
Recipes for serving fruits have already been given, see pages 153–70 and for rice puddings, see pages 176–8.
For Pastry, see Chapter 20, pages 195–201.

Chocolate blancmange puddings

WITH ORANGE. To a 1 pt (½ l) mixture add only half the recommended sugar and stir in the grated yellow rind of:

   1 *large orange*

Pour the cooked mixture into a large mould or four individual ones. When cold and set unmould and garnish with:

   Peeled and sliced fresh orange or with canned mandarin oranges

If liked garnish with:

   Whipped cream or hand thin cream separately

MOCHA MOULD

   1 *pt packet chocolate mould (½ l): 2 tsp soluble coffee: vanilla essence: pinch of salt*

Add the coffee, salt and vanilla to the cooked mould and mix well.

   1 *egg white*

Beat until stiff and fold into the hot chocolate mixture. Pour into a large serving dish or individual dishes.

   Cream

Either garnish with whipped cream or serve thin cream separately. In the case of individual dishes, run a little thin cream on top of each and garnish with a cherry.

CHOCOLATE MOULD WITH FRUIT. Make the mould in the usual way, unmould and serve with stewed or canned fruit. Best fruits with chocolate are oranges, pears, rhubarb and red plums.

CHOCOLATE MOULD WITH RAISINS

2–4 oz seeded raisins (60–120 g): rum or liqueur

Soak the raisins in the rum while making the mould. Stir raisins in at the end, just before pouring into the mould.

CUSTARDS. These need little preparation and can be cooked in four minutes in a pressure cooker or left to cook slowly in the oven. They can be made in advance and stored in the refrigerator for several days.

QUANTITIES for 4

3 eggs: ½ oz sugar (1 Tbs or 15 g): pinch of salt

Beat together just enough to blend egg whites and yolks.

1 pt milk (2 c or ½ l)

Heat the milk and when it is almost boiling pour it into the egg mixture.

Flavouring to taste: grated nutmeg (optional)

Add flavouring to taste. This may be vanilla or other essence, finely grated orange or lemon rind or soluble coffee. Pour the custard into a baking dish and sprinkle the top with nutmeg if liked.

Pressure Cooking

Put the custard mixture in a dish which will go easily into the pressure cooker leaving room to spare all round and on top. Cover with a lid of foil. Put ½ pt (1 c or ¼ l) of hot water in the cooker, put in the trivet and stand the custard on this. Pressure cook at 15 lb pressure for exactly 4 minutes. Allow pressure to reduce slowly before removing the pudding.

Baking

COOKING TIME: 1–1 ½ hrs: TEMPERATURE E 250°, G 1

Put the dish containing the custard in a shallow tin with hot water to come half-way up the sides of the dish. Bake until set. To test this insert a clean knife blade in the custard half-way between the centre and the side. If it comes out clean, the custard is done. Remove immediately from the water and leave to cool.

ICE-CREAM. If commercial ice-cream is purchased in family blocks, wrapped in several layers of newspaper for transport, it can then be transferred to the freezing compartment of the refrigerator and will keep for up to 6 hrs provided it was still firm when put in. In the deep freeze it will keep for several weeks.

There are a number of ready-mix ice-cream powders on the market, some of them very good and they make a basis for adding flavours of your own choice.

Making your own ice-cream does not take long if the following recipes are used. It is important to freeze it as quickly as possible so the refrigerator should be set at its coldest before the ice-cream is put to freeze and the mixture should be well chilled. When the ice-cream is frozen, the control can be turned back to normal until the ice-cream is wanted. It will keep several hours at this setting. If it is not wanted until some time later, it is better to store the ice-cream in a covered box in the deep freeze.

QUICK VANILLA ICE

QUANTITIES for 4–6

½ pt whipping cream (1 c or ¼ l): 1 oz sifted icing sugar (¼ c or 30 g): ½ tsp vanilla essence

Whip the cream and add the vanilla and sugar.

1 *egg white*

Beat until stiff and fold into the cream. Pour into freezing tray and freeze in the refrigerator. It does not need to be stirred during freezing.

QUICK FRUIT ICE

QUANTITIES for 4

¼ pt thick fruit purée (½ c or 1½ dl): 1 oz sifted icing sugar (¼ c or 30 g)

The purée is most quickly made in the electric blender using raw ripe fruit or drained cooked or canned fruit. About ½ lb (250 g) fruit makes ¼ pt (1½ dl) purée. Add the sugar and stir until it is dissolved.

¼ pt whipping cream (½ c or 1½ dl) or ⅛ pt chilled evaporated milk (¼ c or ¾ dl)

Whip the cream or milk until stiff and fold in the fruit.

A little finely grated orange or lemon rind (optional)

Add to the other mixture and pour into freezing tray. Freeze in the refrigerator without stirring.

Best fruits are: Bananas, raspberries, strawberries, loganberries, blackcurrants or apricots.

CHOCOLATE ICE-CREAM

QUANTITIES for 6–8

½ pt whipping cream (1 c or ¼ dl) or 7½ oz chilled evaporated milk (¾ c): 2 oz plain chocolate (60 g): 1 oz sugar (2 Tbs or 30 g)

Melt the chocolate over a very low heat or in a small basin in a pan of hot water. Add the sugar and 2 Tbs of the cream or milk. Stir and warm until the sugar dissolves.

Whip the remaining cream or milk until it is stiff and then whip in the chocolate mixture blending until smooth. Pour into the freezing tray. Freeze in the refrigerator without stirring.

COFFEE ICE-CREAM

QUANTITIES for 6–8

½–1 Tbs soluble coffee: 1 Tbs rum (optional): 1 oz sugar (2 Tbs or 30 g): ½ pt whipping cream (1 c or ¼ l): or 7½ oz chilled evaporated milk (¾ c or 2 dl)

Mix the coffee and sugar with 2 Tbs of the cream or milk. Stir until the sugar is dissolved. Add the rum.

Whip the remaining cream or milk until stiff and fold in the coffee mixture. Pour into the freezing tray. Freeze in the refrigerator without stirring.

MOCHA ICE-CREAM

QUANTITIES for 6–8

2 oz plain chocolate (60 g): *½–1 Tbs soluble coffee:*
½ pt whipping cream (1 c or ¼ l) *or 7½ oz chilled evaporated milk* (¾ c or 2 dl): *½ oz sugar* (1 Tbs)

Soften the chocolate over a very low heat or in a small basin over hot water. Add the coffee, sugar and 2 Tbs of the cream or milk. Stir until the sugar dissolves.

Whip the rest of the cream or milk and beat in the chocolate mixture. Pour into the freezing tray and freeze in the refrigerator without stirring.

WAYS OF SERVING ICE-CREAM

Vanilla ice-cream with hot chocolate sauce
    For sauce, see page 58.
Pears Hélène Stew pears in a vanilla flavoured syrup or use canned pears. Arrange pears on vanilla ice-cream and serve with hot chocolate sauce, see page 58.
Peach Melba Skin ripe peaches and serve on a bed of vanilla ice-cream with Melba sauce. This sauce can be purchased ready made or see recipe, page 61.
Melon and Ginger Coupe Mix diced fresh or canned melon with some chopped crystallised or preserved ginger. Add a portion of vanilla ice-cream and sprinkle with grated chocolate.
Meringue Glacé Join two meringues together with vanilla, chocolate or coffee ice-cream and serve with chopped fresh fruit or fruit salad.
Banana and Blackcurrant Coupe Arrange sliced bananas round a portion of vanilla ice-cream and pour some blackcurrant syrup over it.

Chocolate and Ginger Serve chocolate ice-cream garnished with sliced preserved ginger and whipped cream flavoured with a little ginger syrup.

JELLIES

Ready-prepared jellies are available in many flavours and it is quite easy to make others of your own choice from canned or fresh fruit juices and gelatine using the amounts recommended on the packet. The fresh fruit juices are easy to prepare if you have a juice extractor attachment to your electric mixer or if you own a juice press.

Metal moulds are the best to use for setting jellies and there are many sizes and shapes available. Plastic moulds are satisfactory but do not give quite such a good shape as the metal.

When setting fruit in a jelly allow the jelly to cool until it is just beginning to thicken and then add the fruit.

To speed up the setting stand the mould in a bowl of iced water. This is better than putting a warm jelly into the refrigerator. Cool jelly can be poured into the ice trays of the refrigerator for final speedy setting. It can then be served as chopped jelly. Alternatively, put the jelly in individual moulds small enough to go into the ice-making compartment of the refrigerator.

To unmould a jelly, have a basin of hot water a little deeper than the mould. Loosen the edges of the jelly with a small knife. Dip the mould in the hot water for a moment or two and wipe dry. Twirl and shake until the jelly is loosened. Invert the serving dish over the jelly and turn upside down. Shake to loosen finally.

WAYS OF USING A PACKET JELLY

WITH EGG

Make the jelly according to directions but with 2 Tbs less water. Allow it to become cold but not set and then add 2 beaten eggs. Mix well and strain into the mould.

Alternatively, add the hot jelly. This requires care as the jelly should be really hot yet not boiling so that it cooks the eggs without curdling.

MILK JELLY

Make the jelly up with only half the required amount of water. When it is cold and just beginning to set, gradually stir in evaporated milk in place of the rest of the water. Pour into a mould and leave to set.

CRÊME DE MENTHE JELLY

Colour a lemon jelly pale green or use a lime or greengage jelly. Flavour it to taste with peppermint essence and pour it into a shallow glass dish. Serve it in this dish or break it up into individual dishes. Either decorate with whipped cream or hand single cream separately.

YOGHURT JELLY

For four portions make ½ pt (1 c or ¼ l) any packet jelly and leave it to cool. When it is about to set, add it to ¼ pt yoghurt (1 jar or 1½ dl). Use the electric beater to whisk it until light. Pour into a mould.

PEAR JELLY

Put half a drained canned pear in each individual serving dish, or use very ripe peeled and cored raw pears. Make a lime jelly and pour it over the pears.

WINE OR CIDER JELLY

Make a pint (½ l) lemon jelly leaving out a quarter of the water. In its place use cider, white wine, port or claret. The cider jelly makes a very good basis for setting fruit.

PEACHES IN CIDER JELLY

COOKING TIME: 3–5 mins: QUANTITIES for 4

1 *lb tin of peach halves* (½ *kg*)

Drain the fruit, keeping the syrup. Arrange the peaches in a single layer in a shallow dish or in individual dishes.

1 ½ *Tbs gelatine*

Add to the syrup and warm over a gentle heat until the gelatine is dissolved. Stir occasionally. Remove from the heat and add.

2 *Tbs lemon juice: ½ pt cider (1 c or ¼ l)*

Pour this gently over the fruit and leave to set.

Cream

Hand thin cream separately or pipe with whipped cream.
ALTERNATIVELY Make jelly as in previous recipe for 'Wine or Cider Jelly'.

SEMOLINA WITH ALMONDS (using canned Semolina pudding)

COOKING TIME: 5–10 mins: QUANTITIES for 4

1 *oz butter (2 Tbs or 30 g): 2 oz blanched almonds (60 g)*

Heat the butter in a pan and toss the almonds in it for a minute. Remove.

1 *oz ground almonds (¼ c or 30 g): 2 oz sultanas or raisins (¼ c or 60 g): ¼ tsp ground cloves: ½ tsp ground cinnamon*

Add to the pan and stir and cook for a couple of minutes. Remove from the heat.

1 *lb can of semolina pudding (½ kg)*

Add pudding to the pan and allow to heat through.
Turn into a fireproof dish.

1 *Tbs brown sugar*

Sprinkle on top of the pudding and grill to melt the sugar. Decorate with the almonds and grill again to brown tips. Serve hot or cold.

SPONGE FLANS

These can be made with home-made sponge mixture, see page 210, or a packet sponge mixture. Alternatively, buy a ready-made or deep frozen flan. If you make your own, make extra for the deep freezer as the unfilled flans keep very well. Bake as for Sponge Sandwich.

Fillings

RASPBERRY FLAN

8–12 oz fresh or frozen raspberries (250–375 g): ¼ pt whipping cream (½ c or 1½ dl): sugar to taste

Pick over-fresh raspberries and sprinkle them with castor sugar. If possible do this in advance and leave for some hours in the refrigerator.

For frozen raspberries without sugar, sprinkle with sugar to taste and defrost. Whip the cream, fold in the fruit and pile in the flan case. If there are a few berries of good shape, keep these back to decorate the top.

APRICOT OR PEACH FLAN

1 lb can apricot halves or sliced peaches (½ kg): 4 Tbs red currant jelly

Drain the fruit and arrange it in the flan. Melt the jelly and brush it over the fruit. Decorate with:

Whipped cream

PEAR AND HONEY

1 lb fresh ripe pears or 1 lb canned (½ kg)

If fresh pears are used, peel and quarter them and stew gently in a little syrup. Drain well. Canned fruit should also be drained well. Arrange fruit in flan.

2 Tbs clear honey

If necessary, warm honey to make it flow and then brush over the fruit.

FRUIT SPONGE PUDDING

COOKING TIME: 50 mins: QUANTITIES for 4
TEMPERATURE E 350°, G 4

1 lb fruit, fresh or defrosted (½ kg): 2 oz sugar (4 Tbs or 60 g)

G

Put these in a pie dish.

Packet sponge mix or two-minute cake, see page 213.

Make the sponge or cake and spread it over the fruit. Bake until the sponge is cooked. Stand the dish on a baking tray in case it boils over during cooking.
Serve hot with:

Cream or custard sauce

STEAMED APPLE AND CEREAL PUDDING

COOKING TIME: 1 ½–2 hrs: QUANTITIES for 4
1 ½ lb apples (750 g)

Peel and slice thickly or use frozen sliced ones.

1 ½ oz crumbled weetabix or other wheat breakfast cereal (3 bix or 45 g): 3 oz brown sugar (6 Tbs or 100 g): ¼ tsp salt

Put the apples in layers with these ingredients in a 2 pint basin.

⅛ pt water (¼ c or ¾ dl): more cereal crumbs

Pour in the water. Cover with a layer of crumbs and then with a lid of foil, steam for 1 ½–2 hrs.
Serve in the cooking dish or turn out into another dish.
Serve with:

Cream

BAKED FRUIT AND CEREAL PUDDING

COOKING TIME: 1 hr: TEMPERATURE E 300–325°, G 2–3

Use the above mixture but put it in a pie dish or other oven dish and do not cover during baking.

Suitable fruit would be: apples, blackcurrants, rhubarb, raspberries, stoned and sliced plums. Fruit can be fresh or frozen.

If frozen is used, there is no need to defrost first, just allow a little longer for the cooking.

CHAPTER TWENTY

Pastry, Pies and Flans

In the average household, these are the most popular of all baked goods.

They are available in a very wide selection of ready-prepared pies, tarts and flans as well as ready-made pastry and pastry mixes. From the deep freeze come ready-made pies both sweet and savoury, turnovers, patties, vol-au-vent, sausage rolls and Cornish pasties. The majority of these require cooking. Frozen pastry needs to be defrosted before being rolled out. The frozen puff paste is the most useful as making this is a very time-consuming job and one which requires skill and experience.

The packet pastry mixes need to have water added for mixing and then to be rolled and shaped. A home-made pastry mix only takes minutes to make and can be stored in the refrigerator or cold larder. It has the advantage of being made with more appetising fats than some of the packet variety.

Home-made fruit pies and flans can be stored in the deep freeze. For tips on buying and storing pastry and pies, see pages 29 and 34–5.

Canned and packet pie fillings of all kinds are available. They save a certain amount of preparation of fruit, though frozen fruit is no more trouble to use and is more like a fresh fruit pie. These include blackcurrant, raspberry, rhubarb, loganberry, peach, apple, lemon, bilberry, blackberry, apricot, blackberry and apple, black cherry, red cherry and pineapple. They are best made into plate tarts with pastry top and bottom.

For the busy woman who wants to make pastry from the raw materials, the Quick Mix method is recommended, see pages 196–7.

PASTRY MIX. Will keep several weeks in the refrigerator: 6 oz of the mix will be enough for a 7 in flan and 8–12 oz for a plate tart.

   1 *lb plain flour* (3 *c or* ½ *kg*): 1 *tsp salt*: 8 *oz fat* (250 *g*) (*preferably half lard and half butter*)

Sift the flour and salt into a basin. Have the fat soft, at room temperature, cut it in pieces, add to the flour and mix with the electric mixer at moderate speed until it looks like fine breadcrumbs. Store the mixture in polythene bags or boxes in a cold place. It keeps longest in the refrigerator.

When it is to be used, weigh out the required amount and add water to mix in the proportions of 1–2 Tbs per 6 oz (180 g) of mix.

QUICK MIX SHORT CRUST PASTRY

   8 *oz flour* (1 ½ *c or* 250 *g*): ½ *tsp salt*

Sift into a mixing bowl or into the bowl of the electric mixer.

   4 *oz fat* (½ *c or* 120 *g*) *This can be a mixture of half butter or margarine and half lard or cooking fat*

The fat must be soft. If taken straight out of the refrigerator, put it in a warm place to soften but not melt.

Add fat to flour with 2–3 Tbs cold water and stir with a fork until well blended. In the electric mixer use a moderate speed. Do not add any more water unless absolutely necessary. Roll out and use as required.

QUICK MIX BISCUIT CRUST OR PASTRY

TEMPERATURE E 400°, G 6: QUANTITIES for two 8 in (20 cm) flans

8 oz self-raising flour (1 ½ c or 100 g): pinch of salt

Sift into a mixing bowl.

3 oz softened butter or margarine (6 Tbs or 100 g): 2 oz caster sugar (4 Tbs or 60 g): 1 egg

Add these to the flour and mix for one minute or until well blended, using either an electric mixer on slow speed or hand mixing. Roll out and use as required for flans, plate tarts, jam tarts and other sweet goods.

UNCOOKED PASTRY FLANS. These are simple to make and can be kept in the refrigerator until needed. A heat-resistant glass pie plate is the best utensil in which to make them, but any dish of a similar shape is suitable.

QUANTITIES for 6–7 in pie plate

2 oz butter or margarine (4 Tbs or 60 g): 1 Tbs golden syrup

Melt these together.

3 oz cornflake crumbs (1 c or 100 g): 1 oz brown sugar (2 Tbs or 30 g)

Add to the melted mixture and stir well. Press into the pie plate to make a flan shape. Place in the refrigerator and chill until firm.

FILLINGS for uncooked pastry flans.

1. Use packet pie filling such as lemon, and garnish with fresh fruit or whipped cream
2. Use 12 oz raw, ripe or defrosted frozen raspberries or strawberries (375 g) with ½ pt raspberry or strawberry jelly (¼ l)
3. Use 1 lb stewed or canned fruit (½ kg) and thicken the juice with arrowroot or potato starch using 1 Tbs starch to ½ pt juice (¼ l)

With 2 and 3 arrange the fruit in the flan. If jelly is used, allow it to cool and begin to thicken before spooning it over the fruit. With the thickened juice, pour it over the fruit while it is hot.

WAYS OF USING READY-MADE PUFF PASTRY. This can be bought ready to roll out. If it is frozen, it will have to be left for an hour or so to defrost before rolling. Roll as soon as it is ready to handle.

It is more often used for covering savoury than sweet pies (see Steak and Kidney Pie, page 100), but there is no reason why it should not be used for a fruit pie such as apple or for a double crust tart, as long as it rolled as thinly as possible.

PALMIERS

COOKING TIME: 5–10 mins: TEMPERATURE E 450°, G 8

Puff pastry: caster sugar

Roll the pastry about ⅛ in (3 cm) thick on a board sprinkled with caster sugar instead of flour. Roll it to a rectangle. Fold the sides to the centre and then these folded sides to the centre again. Cut the roll thus formed in slices across, about ¼ in (6 cm) thick. Put the slices on a greased tray or one covered with silicone paper or foil, having the cut sides of the pastry uppermost, and allowing room for a little spreading. Sprinkle them with sugar and bake until they are pale brown. They can be served plain as a biscuit or joined in pairs with:

Whipped cream

PATTIES AND VOL-AU-VENT. These can be purchased ready made from bakers or from the deep freeze but it is quite simple to make them using frozen puff pastry.

COOKING TIME: 15–20 mins: TEMPERATURE E 450°, G 9
QUANTITIES 1 lb pastry (½ kg) makes 8 patties, 3 in (8 cm) diameter or 4 vol-au-vent 6 in (15 cm) diameter

Frozen pastry should be defrosted until it is soft enough to roll but is still firm. Roll it out to about ⅛ in thick. After rolling, lift the pastry up from the board to let air get underneath. This relaxes any stretching the pastry may have had and gives a better shaped patty.

Stamp out rounds of the required size, making a clean sharp cut. With a smaller cutter, stamp out the centres of half the rounds, keeping the centres for caps. Put the plain rounds on a moistened baking tray, moisten them with a pastry brush and press the ring halves on top, making sure they are evenly placed. Put the caps on the tray. Put in a cold place to rest for 20 mins.

When re-rolling trimmings, put the pieces one on top of the other in layers before rolling out.

Brush the rims of the patties and the caps with a little egg mixed with water. Bake until golden brown and set.

Patties are best served hot. They may be made in advance and re-heated but do not add the hot filling until the end.

For suggestions for fillings see Chicken Patties and Vol-au-Vent page 112, and Sea Food Vol-au-Vent, page 222.

APPLE PIE. To save time, use sliced frozen apples and ready-made or ready-mix pastry.

COOKING TIME: 30–45 mins: QUANTITIES for 4–6
TEMPERATURE E 425°, G 6

2 lb cooking apples (1 kg) or 1½ lb ready prepared (750 g): 4 oz sugar (½ c or 120 g): ¼ pt or less of water (½ c or 1½ dl)

The whole apples should be peeled and cored and cut in fairly thick slices. Put them in a 2 pt (1 l) pie dish in layers with the sugar. The apples should come above the level of the top of the dish. Add cold water to come half-way up the apples.

2 cloves or a little grated nutmeg or lemon rind

Add flavouring if liked.

6 oz flour (180 g) made into short crust pastry or use 8–12 oz ready-made or ready-mix (250–375 g)

Roll the pastry about ¼ in (6 mm) thick and about 2 in (5 cm) larger than the top of the pie dish. Place the pastry over the rolling pin and lift it gently on top of the pie taking care not to stretch it.

Then trim the edges of the paste to leave about ½ in (3 mm) over-hang. Fold this under to make the edge level with that of the pie-dish. Dampen the flat rim of the dish and press the pastry onto this. Press round the edge with the prongs of a fork to decorate. Cut a slit in the middle of the pastry, brush with beaten egg or milk. Stand the pie dish on a baking tin and bake the pie until the pastry is lightly browned and the apples tender.

Caster sugar

Sprinkle the pastry with sugar and serve the pie with:

Cream or custard sauce or ice-cream or a piece of cheese

DOUBLE CRUST OR PLATE PIE (Tart)

COOKING TIME: 30–45 mins: QUANTITIES for 8–9 in (20–23 cm) tart
TEMPERATURE E 425°, G 6

6–8 oz flour made into short crust pastry or use ½–¾ lb ready-made or ready-mix (250–375 g)

These pies are always best if the pastry is fairly thin and most satis-factory if made in a heat-resistant glass pie plate in which they can be served. Roll half the pastry into a circle to line the bottom and sides of the plate.

1–1½ lb raw fruit (500–750 g): 4 oz sugar (½ c or 120 g): 2 Tbs flour: or use a canned pie filling

Put the filling in the pastry shell using enough to come level with the top of the dish. Roll the second piece of pastry to cover the top. Moisten the edges with water, press to make a good seal, trim the edges and fold them upwards. Cut several small slits in the top and bake until the pastry is lightly browned and the juice begins to run out of the slits.

It is a wise precaution to put the pie plate on a baking tray in case the juice spills over. It is much easier to wash a tray than to clean syrup off the bottom of the oven.

Best fruits for these pies are apples, raspberries, loganberries, rhubarb, plums and blackcurrants. Apples should be peeled, cored and sliced. Berries picked over, hulls and stalks removed. Cut rhubarb in 1 in (2½ cm) lengths.

BAKED JAM ROLL

COOKING TIME: 30–45 mins: QUANTITIES for 4–6
TEMPERATURE E 425°, G 6–7

12 oz ready-mix or ready-made short crust pastry (375 g): jam

Roll the pastry into an oblong, not more than ⅛ in (3 cm) thick. Spread with a thin layer of jam to within about ½ in (1 cm) of the edges. Moisten edges with water and roll pastry up. Press edges well together and put the roll on a baking tray. Bake until lightly browned. Serve hot either plain or with:

Custard sauce or cream

ALTERNATIVE FILLINGS Lemon curd, chopped apples, sultanas and mixed spice combined with jam or honey mixed with chopped nuts and spice.

CHAPTER TWENTY-ONE

Sandwiches

MANY people regard making sandwiches as a time-consuming, tedious job but that need not be the case if sliced loaves are used with simple fillings and if the butter used for spreading is really soft. Take it out of the refrigerator in good time or else cut it up in pieces and put it in a slightly warm oven or other place to soften but not melt.

READY-PREPARED FILLINGS. A large variety of these is sold at the delicatessen, either by the quarter-pound or else in tins or jars. They include items like: herring, salmon or cod's roe paste; cottage cheese spreads; liver pastes; cheese spreads; anchovy paste; yeast and meat extracts; pates; sliced cold meats; smoked salmon; smoked eel; peanut butter.

OTHER EASY SANDWICH FILLINGS
1. Mashed hard-boiled eggs mixed with salad cream or mayonnaise and a pinch of curry powder.
2. Ditto with French mustard and Worcester sauce instead of curry.
3. Canned dressed crab meat.

4. Flaked canned salmon mixed with chopped cucumber and salad dressing.
5. Thinly sliced fresh cucumber with plenty of salt and pepper.
6. Thinly sliced raw tomatoes seasoned with salt and pepper and a pinch of sugar.
7. Mashed sardines with lemon juice or vinegar and pepper.

STORING SANDWICHES. To keep sandwiches fresh, either wrap them in a polythene bag or in foil, or pack them in a plastic box with a fitting lid. Store in a cold place. If they are to be stored in the freezer, freeze them flat and then stack them according to the fillings. They will keep up to three months, but should not include hard-boiled egg, salad vegetables, salad cream or mayonnaise.

Thaw them for 1–2 hrs before serving.

OPEN SANDWICHES. The basis of these is bread or hard bread spread with butter. The copious filling is arranged on top to look as decorative as possible. Large ones are eaten with knife and fork, small ones can be for a finger snack but need to be one bite size.

They form ideal supper or lunch dishes and one or two substantial ones are enough for a meal. In winter a soup can be served first.

Suggested easy fillings or toppings:

1. A slice of ham garnished with tomato and watercress.
2. Canned or cooked shrimps garnished with lemon and parsley.
3. A slice of ham garnished with spears of canned asparagus and a slice of tomato.
4. Salami sausage garnished with chopped onion and sliced radishes.
5. A slice of cheese garnished with lettuce, radishes or pickles.
6. Smoked salmon paste with a garnish of chopped chives and hard-boiled egg.
7. Salami slices garnished with horseradish sauce and parsley.
8. Sliced smoked eel garnished with hard-boiled egg and chopped chives or onion.
9. Pickled herring fillets with potato salad and pickled beetroot.

10. Hard-boiled egg with mayonnaise flavoured with curry powder, lettuce garnish.

11. Small portion of lobster with mayonnaise in a lettuce cup.

12. Slice of roast lamb garnished with cucumber.

13. Slice of roast beef garnished with potato salad and mustard pickles.

14. Slice of roast pork with pickled cucumber and tomato.

CHAPTER TWENTY-TWO

Drinks, Hot and Cold

MOST drinks are available in easy-to-prepare forms. If you keep a basic store of the kinds you like and replenish them before they have run out, this will be a trouble-free branch of your catering. For tips on buying and storing see pages 23 and 34.

Choose from this list for your basic store
Dried and evaporated milk
Drinking chocolate and/or cocoa
Coffee beans or ground coffee and soluble coffee
Tea, leaf or instant
Yeast or meat extracts
Bottled, canned, dried or frozen fruit juices: orange, grapefruit pineapple, apple, guava
Fruit squashes
Lime juice
Ginger ale
Bitter lemon
Soda water

Tonic water
Fruit syrups: blackcurrant, cherry, raspberry, etc.
Canned lemon juice
Coca-Cola
Lemon barley water
Canned and bottled tomato juice or tomato cocktail
Canned vegetable juices
Horlicks, Ovaltine, Nesquick, Milo

Basic store of alcoholic drinks

Sherry	Dry and Sweet white wine
Beer	Whisky
Red wine	Brandy
Gin	Vermouth
Cider	One or two liqueurs

TO MAKE A GOOD CUP OF TEA

Allow 1–2 tsp tea per cup and 1–2 over for the pot

Use freshly drawn water from the cold tap and have it freshly boiled. Just before the kettle boils use a little of the water to rinse out and warm the teapot. Throw this away.

Alternatively, put the pot in a warm place to heat up.

Add the tea and take the pot to the boiling kettle, pouring the water in as soon as it boils. Put on the lid and allow the tea to stand for 3–8 mins before using. A tea with fine leaves needs less time to brew than a large leafed tea. Stir well before pouring out. When milk is taken, it is put in the cup before the tea. Tea without milk is usually made weaker and served with slices of lemon.

TO MAKE A GOOD CUP OF COFFEE

Allow 4 Tbs coffee to ½ pt water (1 c or ¼ l)

The two simplest ways of making coffee are to use either a percolator or a vacuum type of coffee maker (Cona). Failing either of these, make it in a jug, but you need some means of keeping the jug hot and of heating the coffee pot into which it will be strained. Put the coffee in the warmed brewing jug and pour in the measured amount of boiling water. Stir and draw a spoon across the top to remove any floating grounds. Stand to keep hot but not boiling for 3–4 mins. Strain through a fine meshed strainer into a heated coffee pot.

USING A VACUUM TYPE COFFEE POT
Fine or medium ground coffee is suitable. Put the water in the lower compartment and the coffee in the top. When the water boils it siphons up into the top. Stir well and keep the heat on for 1 min for a fine grind and 3 mins for a medium grind. Remove from the heat and wait for the coffee to come down to the lower bowl. Remove the top container and serve the coffee.

PERCOLATED COFFEE
Use fine or medium ground coffee in the proportions given above. When the water begins to percolate, time for 5–8 mins depending on the strength required.

TO MAKE COCOA.
Many people find drinking chocolate too sweet for their taste and the alternative is to make cocoa:
Allow per cup:

> 2 tsp cocoa powder: 1 tsp sugar: 1 or more Tbs dried milk powder: pinch of salt: 8 oz water (2 dl)

Mix the dry ingredients to a paste with a little cold water, add the rest boiling.

To improve the flavour, put the cocoa in a small pan and boil for 1–2 mins.

If liked, beat to make frothy and add a little vanilla essence.

ALTERNATIVE Omit the dried milk and use some fresh or evaporated. Or make entirely with fresh hot milk.

QUICK MILK DRINKS IN THE ELECTRIC BLENDER
Simply put all ingredients in the blender and mix until smooth.
QUANTITIES for 1 drink

BANANA MILK SHAKE

> 8 oz milk (2 dl): 1 small ripe banana, skinned

ICED COFFEE

¼ *pt water* (½ *c or* 1½ *dl*): 2 *tsp instant coffee or to taste:* 1 *Tbs cream:* 2 *Tbs instant dried milk:* 1 *oz ice-cream* (30 *g*)

If no ice-cream is available, chill after mixing.

EGG NOG

1 *egg:* 1–2 *tsp sugar:* ¼ *pt hot or cold milk* (½ *c or* 1½ *dl*): *vanilla:* 1 *tsp brandy or sherry: grated nutmeg*

TOMATO MILK DRINK

2 *tomatoes:* ⅛ *pt water* (¼ *c or* 1 *dl*): ½ *oz instant milk powder* (2 *Tbs or* 15 *g*): ½ *tsp celery salt*

TOMATO CHEESE

¼ *pt chilled tomato juice* (½ *c or* 1½ *dl*): 2 *oz cottage cheese* (60 *g*): *pinch of celery salt: more salt to taste*

BANANA AND PINEAPPLE

2 *oz peeled ripe banana* (60 *g*): ½ *oz instant milk powder* (2 *Tbs or* 15 *g*): ¼ *pt canned pineapple juice* (½ *c or* 1½ *dl*)

LEMONADE OR ORANGEADE

QUANTITIES for about 2 pt

2 *lemons or* 1 *lemon and* 1 *orange or grapefruit:* 1¾ *pt cold water* (3½ *c or* 1 *l*): 1–2 *oz sugar to taste* (2–4 *Tbs or* 30–60 *g*)

Scrub the fruit and cut in small pieces.

Put in the blender with the other ingredients and mix for a few seconds to break into a coarse pulp.

Strain at once and chill.

ICED TEA

Strain hot, strong tea into glasses one-third full of small ice cubes. Add sugar and lemon juice to taste and a thin slice of lemon per glass.

ALTERNATIVE Make average or weakish tea. Add sugar and lemon juice to taste. Cool and then chill in the refrigerator.

Serve with a slice of lemon.

USING AN ELECTRIC JUICE EXTRACTOR. With this, any fresh fruit or vegetables can be used to give a liquid. A single fruit can be used or a mixture. The following are some suggestions:

QUANTITIES are per drink.

FRUIT AND PARSLEY JUICE

½ oz parsley (15 g): 1 small peeled orange: ½ peeled lemon: 1 apple cut in pieces

Put in the juice extractor.

½ peeled banana

Mash and add to the drink just before serving.

APPLE AND LEMON

8 oz apple, cut up (250 g): ¼ peeled lemon, cut up: sugar to taste

Put apple and lemon in the juice extractor. Sweeten juice to taste.

CARROTS AND ORANGE

8 oz young washed carrots, (250 g) cut up: 4 oz apples (120 g) washed and cut up: 4 oz celery, washed and cut up (120 g): ½ peeled lemon cut up

Put in the extractor and chill the juice before serving.

CHAPTER TWENTY-THREE

Cakes are Easier than you Think

You can, of course, buy them ready made. If you want something elaborate and special, this is the best thing to do as this sort of cake demands experience, skill and time to make well.

Ready-mixes are available in great variety and are quick and easy to use and the best solution, if you want to serve cake frequently. Most of them only use one egg per cake and get their main lightness with a large amount of raising agent incorporated in the mix. This usually produces a typical flavour which some find objectionable.

If you have an electric mixer, there are many cakes which are quick and easy to make and enable you to use better quality ingredients than the average ready-mix. A selection of recipes for this type of cake are given here and some suggestions which can also be used with ready-mixes.

For tips on buying and storing see page 23.

GENOESE SPONGE. A delicious cake requiring no raising agent other than the eggs. It keeps very well, even deep frozen and is easy to make with an electric mixer.

COOKING TIME: 25–30 mins: TEMPERATURE E 375°, G 5

QUANTITIES for a 10 in (25 cm) x 8 in (20 cm) tin or two 7 in (18 cm) sandwich tins

Use non-stick tins or line the bottom with a piece of non-stick silicone paper, or foil.

3 large eggs: 4 oz caster sugar (½ c or 120 g)

If the eggs have come straight out of the refrigerator or cold larder, break them into the mixing bowl and stand this in a basin of warm water until the bowl is well heated. Add the sugar and beat on fast speed until the mixture is very thick. That means that when the beaters are lifted out the mixture takes a few seconds to fill the depression left. This is the secret of success.

3 oz plain flour (⅔ c or 100 g): 1 Tbs cornflour: 3 oz melted butter (6 Tbs or 100 g)

While the eggs are beating, warm the butter to melt it but do not allow it to become hot. Sift the flour and cornflour into the eggs and mix on slow speed just until the flour is incorporated. Then add the melted butter and mix again. Pour into the prepared tins and bake until the centre feels springy when tested lightly with finger pressure and when the cake has begun to shrink from the sides of the tin.

Leave for 10–15 mins and then turn out onto a cake rack to cool.

WAYS OF USING

Just plain fingers of this are delicious with a fruit salad or at tea time. It can be made into a sponge sandwich with jam or other filling or whipped cream. Serve as a sweet with whipped cream piled on top of a single layer of the cake and decorate with fresh ripe or defrosted fruit.

Use in any recipe requiring a sponge mixture.

AFGHANS

COOKING TIME: 20 mins: QUANTITIES for 24 cakes:
TEMPERATURE E350°, G 4

6 oz plain flour (1¼ c or 180 g): ¼ tsp salt: 1 oz cocoa (3 Tbs or 30 g)

Sift these into a mixing bowl.

> 3 *oz sugar* (6 *Tbs or* 100 *g*): 2 *oz cornflakes* (2 *c or* 60 *g*): 7 *oz melted butter* (14 *Tbs or* 200 *g*): *vanilla essence*

Add to the flour and mix well. Drop small spoonfuls on an oiled or non-stick tray and bake until firm.

OPTIONAL DECORATION

> *Choclate icing: halves of walnuts*

When cold, drop a blob of icing on top of each and decorate with a half walnut. Use ready-mix icing.

MERINGUES. These are very quick and easy to make, taste much better than ready-made, and the mixture can be used in a variety of ways for cakes and sweets. If the meringues are well dried during baking, they will keep for several weeks in an airtight container.

COOKING TIME: 1 hr or more: QUANTITIES for 18 meringues: TEMPERATURE E 250–275°, G ¼–½

> 2 *egg whites*

Crack the eggs by tapping with a sharp knife, put thumbs in crack to separate, tilting the shell so that the yolk stays in one half and the white falls into the mixing bowl. Tilt yolk gently backwards and forwards from one half of the shell to the other until all the white is separated. Should a bit of yolk escape with the white it must be removed. Do this with a piece of the shell.
Beat the egg whites on high speed until the mixture will stand up in peaks.

> 4 *oz caster or granulated sugar* (½ *c or* 120 *g*): *vanilla essence or other flavouring (see below)*

Add half the sugar to the eggs, using caster for a fine texture and granulated for a crunchy texture. Beat again until the mixture is very thick. Add the rest of the sugar and the flavouring at slow speed, mixing just long enough to incorporate. Place spoonfuls on oiled trays or on sheets of silicone-treated paper or foil on trays. Bake until they are completely dried and crisp.

To test, lift one out and press the bottom with your thumb and it should be firm. If it is still squashy, the meringues need longer to dry out.

VARIATIONS

1. *Coffee Meringues* Add 1–1½ tsp soluble coffee for flavouring. Shape as above or spread the mixture on two circles of foil, about 6 in (15 cm) diameter. When cooked and cold, sandwich with whipped cream or ice-cream and fresh or defrosted fruit. Serve as cake or sweet.

2. *Lemon Meringue* Add the finely grated rind of 1 lemon for the flavouring.

3. *Cornflake Meringue* Add 2 oz (2 c or 60 g) cornflakes to the mixture and bake in small heaps until crisp. Some chopped nuts and glacé cherries can be added to this.

4. *Meringue for Topping* a pudding or baked fruit. The basic mixture can be used or one with 2–3 oz sugar (60–100 g) according to taste. Bake at about E 300–350°, G 3–4, until lightly coloured. It is not meant to be dried out and crisp.

5. *Almond Meringue* Make the plain meringues and, just before baking, sprinkle the tops with flaked almonds. When cooked, join in pairs with whipped cream.

TWO MINUTE CAKE-MIX

COOKING TIME: 20–30 mins : TEMPERATURE E 375°, G 5
QUANTITIES for two 7 in (18 cm) sandwich tins

Grease and flour the tins or line the bottoms with non-stick paper or foil.

6 oz self-raising flour (1 c + 3 Tbs or 180 g): pinch of salt

Sift these into a mixing bowl.

3 eggs: 6 oz caster sugar (¾ c or 180 g): 2 Tbs milk: 3 oz butter (6 Tbs or 100 g) melted but not hot

Add these to the flour and mix or beat with a wooden spoon or on the slow speed of an electric mixer for 2 mins or until smooth. Spread evenly in the tins and bake until it feels springy when tested by pressing with a finger. Leave in the tins for 15 mins and then turn out on a rack to cool.

When cold, fill with jam or other cake filling. It will keep for about a week in an airtight tin and deep freezes very well.

OTHER SUGGESTIONS FOR USING

Use in place of sponge mixtures for puddings, upside-down cake and so on.

One half of the cake can be used piled with whipped cream and fresh or canned fruit and the other put in the deep freeze for storing. It is also a suitable mixture for cutting up to make individual fancy cakes.

SMALL MARZIPAN CAKES

Sponge mixture

Make any plain sponge mixture and bake it in one flat tin or two sandwich tins. When it is cold, cut out rounds of the mixture with a 1½–2 in (4–5 cm) diameter plain cutter.

MARZIPAN *Use about ½ lb (250 g) ready made or mix the following together:*

> 4 oz ground almonds (1 c or 120 g): 2 oz icing sugar (½ c or 60 g): 2 oz castor sugar (¼ c or 60 g): 1 egg yolk: 1 tsp lemon juice: few drops almond and vanilla essence

This will be enough for about 8 small cakes. Roll it out thinly and cut strips wide enough to go round the sides of the cakes and stamp out enough rounds for the tops.

Apricot jam

Thin some jam with a little hot water and brush the sides of the cake with it. Wrap a piece of marzipan round each, brush the tops and put a round of marzipan on each.

Glacé cherries

Press half a cherry onto the centre of each.

UPSIDE-DOWN CAKE

COOKING TIME: ½–¾ hr: TEMPERATURE E 350–375°, G 4–5
QUANTITIES for a tin approx 6 in (15 cm) x 9 in (23 cm) or one 8 in (20 cm) diameter

1 *oz butter* (2 *Tbs or* 30 *g*): *canned, fresh or crystallised fruit. fine brown sugar*

Melt the butter in the baking tin and tip to coat evenly. Sprinkle in a thick layer of brown sugar. Drain canned fruit and arrange pieces of fruit to make a pattern on the sugar. Best fruits to use are pineapple, apricots, peaches, crystallised or glacé fruits and nuts.

A packet sponge mix the size to make a 7 in (18 *cm*) *sandwich, or use* TWO MINUTE CAKE-MIX *recipe, see page* 213.

Make the cake and spread it evenly and gently over the fruit. Bake until a skewer inserted in the middle comes out clean. Turn the cake upside down on a serving dish. Serve as a cake or as a pudding with cream handed separately.

This deep freezes very well. Thaw at room temperature before serving.

CHOCOLATE CRISPIES
These are very quick and easy.

COOKING TIME: 10 mins: TEMPERATURE: E 375°, G 5
QUANTITIES for 24 cakes

6 *oz bitter chocolate* (180 *g*)

Melt this in a basin over a pan of hot water or in a pan over a very low heat.

½ *pt sweetened condensed milk* (1 *c or* ¼ *l*)

Add to the chocolate and heat gently for 5 mins or until the mixture thickens. Cool.

3½ *oz cornflakes* (3½ *c or* 100 *g*)

Stir these into the chocolate mixture. Place in spoonfuls on an oiled or non-stick tray and bake. Remove onto a rack to cool.

When cold, store in an airtight container.

ROLLED OAT FINGERS
COOKING TIME: 25–30 mins: TEMPERATURE E 350°, G 4
QUANTITIES for 18 fingers

8 *oz rolled oats* (2 *c or* 250 *g*): *pinch of salt:* 3 *oz soft brown sugar* (6 *Tbs or* 100 *g*): 2 *oz chopped nuts (optional)* (½ *c or* 60 *g*)

Combine these in a mixing bowl

   5 *oz butter* (10 *Tbs or* 150 *g*)

Melt butter and add it to the other ingredients and mix well. Tip the crumbly mixture into an oiled swiss roll tin and spread it out evenly. Bake until the sides are just beginning to colour. Mark into fingers and leave in the tin to cool.

FUDGE FINGERS

   QUANTITIES for 18 fingers

   2 *Tbs syrup or honey:* 2 *oz brown sugar* (4 *Tbs or* 60 *g*): ¼ *tsp salt:* 2 *oz butter* (4 *Tbs or* 60 *g*): 1–2 *oz cocoa* (¼–½ *c or* 30–60 *g*)

Heat these in a pan until butter and sugar are melted. Use the larger amount of cocoa if you like a strong bitter chocolate flavour.

   1 *Tbs rum*

Stir into the mixture.

   4 *oz cornflake crumbs* (1 ⅓ *c or* 120 *g*)

Add to the mixture and stir until blended. Spread evenly in a 6–7 in (15–18 cm) sandwich tin and leave to set.

   9 *walnut halves*

Before cooling, press a quarter of a walnut at intervals round the edge and mark the mixture into small pieces. *Alternatively*, the mixture may be iced with a chocolate covering and decorated to taste.

CREAM CHEESE ICING

   3 *oz cream cheese* (100 *g*): *juice of* 1 *lemon*

Beat these together until the mixture is smooth.

   Fine brown sugar

Beat in sugar until the mixture is of a spreading consistency.
   Use as a filling and/or icing.

QUICK-MIX GINGERBREAD. Serve this warm as a pudding with whipped cream, or cold as a cake. It keeps well in an airtight tin and longer still in the deep freeze.

COOKING TIME: 45 mins: TEMPERATURE E 350°, G 4
QUANTITIES for a tin about 9 in (23 cm) square. Line bottom with non-stick paper.

8 oz plain flour (1 ½ c or 250 g) or use half white and half wholemeal: 1 tsp mixed spice: pinch salt: 1 Tbs ground ginger

Sift these into a mixing bowl, using the electric mixer for easy blending. If wholemeal flour is used, do not sift this but add it afterwards.

2 oz sultanas (⅓ c or 60 g): 1 oz chopped peel or crystallised ginger (2 Tbs or 30 g): 1 ½ oz brown sugar (3 Tbs or 45 g)

Add to the other ingredients.

1 egg: 1 tsp bicarbonate soda: ¼ pt milk (½ c or 1 ½ dl): 4 oz butter or margarine (½ c or 120 g): 8 oz golden syrup or honey (8 Tbs or 250 g)

Melt fat and syrup or honey but do not allow to become hot. Mix soda and milk until the soda dissolves. Add these, together with the egg, to the dry ingredients and mix at slow speed for 1–2 mins or until well blended. Pour into the tin and bake until springy in the centre. Cool for 10–15 mins in the tin and then turn out onto a rack. When quite cold, store in an airtight box or in a suitable container in the deep freeze.

QUICK-MIX CHOCOLATE SANDWICH

COOKING TIME: 25–30 mins: TEMPERATURE E 350°, G 4
QUANTITIES for two 7 in (18 cm) tins. Line bottoms with a circle of non-stick paper

6 oz plain flour (1 ¼ c or 180 g): 1 tsp baking powder: 2 Tbs cocoa powder: ¼ tsp salt

Sift these into the mixing bowl.

4 oz caster sugar (1 ½ c or 120 g)

Add to the flour and mix. Make a well in the centre of these ingredients.

    2 oz butter or margarine (4 Tbs or 60 g): 2 Tbs golden syrup

Melt but do not allow to become hot. Pour into the well.

    1 egg: 1 tsp bicarbonate soda: ¼ pt milk (½ c or 1½ dl): ½ tsp vanilla essence

Add egg to rest of ingredients. Mix soda with the milk and add it; add vanilla. Mix on slow speed of the electric mixer or by hand with a wooden spoon until the mixture is smooth and well blended. Pour into the prepared tins and bake until it feels springy in the middle. Leave for 10 mins and then turn out on a cake rack to cool. When cold store in an airtight box or put in the deep freeze. It may be filled with jam, lemon curd, whipped cream, chocolate icing or any filling liked.

    It may also be served as a pudding with hot chocolate sauce or whipped cream or serve one half of the cake piled with whipped cream and fresh or canned fruit, e.g. canned mandarin oranges.

QUICK MIX FRUIT CAKE

COOKING TIME: 3 hrs: TEMPERATURE E 275–300°, G 1–2
QUANTITIES for an 8 in (20 cm) tin. Line with non-stick paper or foil.

    8 oz plain flour (1½ c or 250 g): 1 tsp baking powder: ½ tsp salt: 1 tsp mixed spice

Sift these into the mixing bowl.

    6 oz fine dark brown sugar (¾ c or 180 g): 3 oz ground almonds (¾ c or 100 g)

Add to the flour and mix. Make a well in the centre of the flour.

    3 eggs: 5 oz softened butter (10 Tbs or 150 g): 2 Tbs milk

Put these in the well and mix into the flour until smooth, using the electric mixer if possible.

    1½ lb mixed dried fruit (4 c or 750 g)

Add to the cake mixture and combine thoroughly. Put into the prepared tin and smooth the top flat.

Blanched almonds

Cover the top with almonds and bake until a fine skewer, inserted in the middle, comes out clean. Leave in the tin to cool. Turn out of the tin and when it is quite cold, store the cake in an airtight box or tin. For longer storage, cut it in portions, pack these in a suitable box and store in the freezer. It should keep for up to 12 months. Defrost in the box, allowing the cake to come to room temperature before serving.

CHAPTER TWENTY-FOUR

Dinner Party Specials

THE following five menus are suggestions for entertaining with the minimum expenditure of time.

Each menu includes a list of ingredients required, a suggested scheme of work including advance preparation, and the necessary recipes.

MENU 1

Mortadella Sausage or Liver Pâté
Toast

*

Sea-Food Vol-au-Vent
Green Peas

*

Fresh Pineapple and Kirsch

*

Cheese and Biscuits

*

Coffee

QUANTITIES for 6

Check list of ingredients

4–8 oz Mortadella sausage or liver pâté (120–250 g).
Stale sliced bread for toast.
Butter.
6 ready-made puff pastry cases or 1 lb prepared puff pastry (½ kg).
3½–4 oz can of oysters (100–120 g).
3½–4 oz can of shrimps (100–120 g).
2 oz can of button mushrooms (60 g).
½ pt milk (¼ l).
White roux.
1 egg.
1 lemon.
2 Tbs cream.
Parsley.
1½ lb fresh or frozen green peas (750 g).
1 large pineapple.
6 Tbs kirsch.
Cheese.
Biscuits or rolls.
Coffee.
Milk and/or cream for the coffee.
Caster sugar and coffee sugar.

Pre-Preparation

1. If you are going to make the vol-au-vent or patty cases yourself, make them the night before and re-heat when required. For the method of rolling and shaping see page 198.
2. The filling can be made in advance if this is more convenient. Cool it quickly and then store in the refrigerator. Re-heat to boiling when required, see recipe page 222.
3. Wash, dry and chop the parsley and store in a polythene bag in the refrigerator.

The rest of the meal is quick and easy to prepare.

Meal Preparation

1. If the filling for the vol-au-vent has not already been made, do this first.

2. Set the table. Put out serving dishes and arrange to heat those needed for serving hot food.

3. Put out the cheese and biscuits and butter.

4. Put out individual portions of the sausage or pâté.

5. Put the peas to cook and the patties to heat.

6. Prepare the pineapple, see below and make the toast.

7. Dish up the main course and put it to keep hot.

8. Make the coffee at the end of the meal.

SEA-FOOD FILLING

3½–4 oz can of oysters (100–120 g): *2 oz can of button mushrooms* (60 g)

Open the cans, drain and keep the liquid.

3½–4 oz can of shrimps (100–120 g)

Open the can and drain.

Milk

Make up the oyster stock to ½ pt (1 c or ¼ l) with milk. Heat.

1½ oz white roux (45 g) (*see page* 54)

Add roux to thicken the sauce, stirring all the time until smooth. Add fish and mushrooms. Cook for 2–3 mins longer.

1 egg yolk: juice of ½ lemon: 2 Tbs cream

Combine these and stir them into the sauce. Do not allow to boil again.

1 Tbs chopped parsley

Add to the sauce. Put the mixture in the hot patties and serve with the boiled green peas.

PINEAPPLE. Slice the pineapple and cut off all skin. Put the slices in individual dishes, sprinkling each piece with caster sugar. Pour Kirsch over the top and serve.

MENU 2

Turtle Soup with Madeira
Toast or Fresh Rolls

*

Roast Veal with Orange Sauce
Roast or Boiled Potatoes
Frozen Peas or Broccoli or Spinach

*

Fresh or Frozen Strawberries or Raspberries
Cream

*

Cheese and Biscuits

*

Coffee
Petits Fours

QUANTITIES for 6

Check list of ingredients

2–3 cans real turtle soup (allow 6–8 oz per portion 180–250 g).
2–3 Tbs Madeira.
Sliced bread for toast or serve fresh rolls.
3½–4 lb piece of veal to roast (2 kg).
Piece of pork fat or fat bacon for the top.
2 oranges.
3 lb old potatoes (1½ kg).
A little milk and butter for the creamed potatoes.
1½ lb vegetables (750 g).
1½ lb strawberries or raspberries (750 g).
½ pt single cream (¼ l).
Caster sugar.
Cheese.
Biscuits and rolls.
Coffee, sugar, milk or cream.
Petits fours.

Pre-Preparation

1. The potatoes can be peeled in advance and covered with cold water.
2. If fresh fruit is used, wash and drain, pick over and remove hulls. Put in a bowl and sprinkle the fruit with caster sugar, cover and store in the refrigerator. Serve in a bowl or in individual portions. Frozen fruit must be taken out of the freezer in time to thaw.

Meal Preparation

1. Put veal and potatoes to roast, using the auto-timer if convenient.
2. Set the table. Put out serving dishes and arrange to heat those required for serving hot food.
3. Put out the cheese and biscuits or rolls, butter, cream in a jug and the petits fours.
4. Fifteen minutes before the meal is to be ready, put the vegetables to cook.
5. Heat the soup and add 2–3 Tbs Madeira just before serving. Make the toast.
6. Dish up the meat and carve it. Put the sauce in a hot sauce boat and put meat and vegetables to keep hot.
7. Make the coffee at the end of the meal.

Cooking the meat and potatoes

The veal will take 40 mins per lb (½ kg) at E 325°, G 3 but let the auto-timer take care of that. Put the meat in the roasting pan with the piece of fat on top. Alternatively, put a piece of foil lightly on top but do not cover completely with foil and do not press down. To use fat is better than foil because it adds flavour. Time the meat to have it cooked a good 15 mins before serving time. Dry the potatoes, brush with oil to coat well and put them round the meat or in a separate pan.

Making the gravy

Remove the meat and put to keep hot. Carefully pour off the fat but retain juices and sediment. Add the juice of 2 oranges and mix and heat stirring to dissolve all the brown sediment. Pour into a heated sauce boat.

MENU 3

Potted Shrimps
Brown Bread and Butter
Lemon Wedges

*

Curried Chicken and Rice
Chutney
Cucumber and Tomato Salad

*

Caramel Oranges and Cream

*

Cheese and Biscuits

*

Coffee

QUANTITIES for 6

Check list of ingredients

2 large or 6 small cartons potted shrimps.
Small sliced loaf brown bread.
Butter.
1 lettuce heart.
2 lemons.
6 pieces roasting chicken.
2 cans Indian curry paste (7½–8 oz size or 250 g).
Oil for frying.
12 oz quick cooking long grain rice (375 g).
1 jar mango chutney.
1 cucumber.
12 oz tomatoes (375 g).
French dressing.
Chopped parsley or tarragon.
6 large oranges.
Liqueur (optional).
Granulated sugar and caster sugar.
Chopped nuts.
¼ pt double (1½ dl) and ¼ pt single cream (1½ dl).

H

Cheeses.
Biscuits.
Coffee.
Milk and/or cream for coffee.

Pre-Preparation
1. Make the caramel oranges the night before and store in the refrigerator. Add cream the next day.
2. Wash and drain the lettuce and store in the refrigerator.
3. If frozen chicken is used, make sure it is defrosted in time, likewise the potted shrimps.
4. The actual cooking of the chicken will take about 1 hour and in that time you can easily assemble and prepare the rest of the meal.

Meal preparation
1. One hour before the meal is required, prepare the chicken curry, see page 227.
2. Set the table: put out serving dishes and arrange to heat those for serving hot food.
3. Put out the cheese and biscuits, butter and the chutney.
4. Make the salad, see page 227.
5. Fifteen minutes before the meal is required, put the rice to cook, see page 227.
6. Whip the cream and use it to decorate the oranges.
7. Serve the shrimps, see page 227.
8. Dish the curry and rice and put to keep hot.
9. Make the coffee at the end of the meal.

CARAMEL ORANGES

COOKING TIME: 5 mins: QUANTITIES for 6

6 large oranges: liqueur (optional): caster sugar

Peel the oranges removing all pith. Cut in slices and remove pips. Put the slices in overlapping rows in a heat-resistant serving dish. Sprinkle with a little sugar and the alcohol.

4 oz granulated sugar (1 ½ c or 120 g): 4 Tbs water

Heat these in a small pan, stirring until the sugar is dissolved. Boil rapidly, without stirring, until the syrup turns a deep amber colour.

Pour it over the oranges and leave in a cold place overnight. The caramel will melt and make a sauce for the oranges.

Whipped cream: chopped nuts

Mix single and double cream and whip. Put on top of the oranges and decorate with chopped nuts.

CURRIED CHICKEN

COOKING TIME: 1 hr: QUANTITIES for 6

6 pieces roasting chicken: oil for frying

Wash and dry the chicken and brown it on both sides in hot oil.

2 cans Indian curry paste (7–8 oz size or 200–250 g) or use 1 pt (½ l) home made curry sauce from the deep freeze

Add the sauce to the chicken, cover and simmer until the chicken is tender.

COOKING THE RICE

12 oz quick cooking long grain rice (1½ c or 375 g): 1½ pt water (3 c or 8 dl): 1 tsp salt

Mix rice, water and salt and bring to the boil. Stir, cover and simmer until all the water is absorbed. Fluff up lightly with a fork and serve.

CUCUMBER AND TOMATO SALAD. Peel and slice the cucumber. Wash and slice the tomatoes. Put them in rows in a shallow dish. Add a pinch of sugar and the French dressing. Sprinkle with chopped parsley or tarragon.

POTTED SHRIMPS Put these out on individual plates with a lettuce leaf under the shrimps. Add wedges of lemon.

The brown bread can be buttered and cut diagonally to give triangular pieces which are then arranged on a plate in overlapping rows, or serve the bread and butter separately.

MENU 4

*

Vichyssoise

*

Baked Ham with Treacle and Cider or Stout
Spinach or Broccoli
Boiled New Potatoes or Potato Purée

*

Apple Purée with Chocolate
Sweet Biscuits

*

Cheese and Biscuits
Coffee

QUANTITIES for 6

Check list of ingredients

2 cans Vichyssoise soup.
Toast or rolls or bread.
3–4 lb piece of gammon or boiling bacon (1 ½–2 kg).
1 Tbs black treacle.
½ pt dry cider or stout (¼ l).
2–3 pkts frozen spinach or broccoli.
3 lb new or old potatoes (1 ½ kg) or 6 portions packet potato powder.
A little milk and butter for mashed potatoes.
1 pt (½ l) apple sauce or purée (2 lb raw apples or 1 kg).
¼ pt double (1 ½ dl) and ¼ pt single cream (1 ½ dl).
2–4 oz grated chocolate (60–120 g).
1 orange.
Glacé cherries.
Sweet biscuits, e.g. chocolate fingers, shortbread.
Coffee.
Cheese and biscuits.
Cream and/or milk for the coffee.

Pre-Preparation
1. Put tins of soup to chill.
2. If the ham is salty, put it to soak in cold water overnight or for several hours.

3. If raw potatoes are used, peel them and put to soak in cold water to cover.

4. If raw apples are used, stew them and make the purée in the blender or by sieving see page 159. If sieving is used, the apples need not be peeled and cored before cooking. Add grated orange rind and sugar to the purée to taste and put to chill.

Meal preparation
1. Put the ham to cook, using the auto-timer if convenient.
2. Set the table, putting out the serving dishes and arrange to heat those to be used for serving hot food.
3. Put out the cheese and biscuits, butter and sweet biscuits.
4. Forty minutes before the meal time, put raw potatoes to cook, see page 230. (Packet potato powder do later.)
5. Finish the sweet, see page 230.
6. Ten minutes before the meal time put the broccoli or spinach to cook.
7. Dish up the meat, carve it and arrange on a serving dish. Put the gravy in a hot sauce boat. Put all this course to keep hot.
8. Serve the soup.
9. Make the coffee at the end of the meal.

BAKED HAM (see also page 95)

COOKING TIME: 30 mins per lb: QUANTITIES allow 4 oz per portion: TEMPERATURE E 325°, G 3

If the bacon has been soaked, drain and put it in fresh water to cover. Bring to the boil and cook for half the required time. Drain and put in the baking dish. Pieces of specially prepared bacon do not need this preliminary boiling and can go straight in the oven.

1 Tbs black treacle: ½ pt dry cider or stout (1 c or ¼ l)

Remove any bacon rind. Spread the treacle over the top of the bacon and pour the liquid round it. Bake, basting occasionally with the liquid. This is not essential and may be omitted if the auto-timer is used.

Serve the bacon or ham sliced with some of the liquor poured over it.

POTATOES Allow ¾ hr if starting to make mashed potatoes from the raw state. Boil until tender, drain and put through ricer or sieve. Return to the pan and beat with a knob of butter and milk to make the desired consistency. Be sure it is hot when served.

Packet potatoes, prepare according to the maker's directions.

APPLE AND CHOCOLATE SWEET. Put the sweetened, flavoured and chilled apple purée in individual serving dishes.

Mix the two creams and whip them, flavouring with a little rum or liqueur if liked.

Spread the cream over the apples and then add a layer of grated chocolate.

Garnish with cherries.

MENU 5

Chicken Consommé with Sherry or Marsala
Toast or Bread

＊

Baked Salmon Steaks en Papillote
Hollandaise Sauce
Boiled Potatoes (New if possible)
Green Peas

＊

Fresh Fruit Flan
Cream

＊

Cheese and Biscuits

＊

Coffee

QUANTITIES for 6

Check list of ingredients

Chicken consommé cubes to make 2 pints (1 l).
6 Tbs sherry or marsala.

Toast or bread.
Butter.
6 salmon steaks, fresh or frozen (about 6–8 oz each or 180–250 g).
2 lemons.
3 egg yolks.
Parsley.
3 lb potatoes (1 ½ kg).
1 ½ lb frozen or fresh shelled peas (750 g).
Flan case.
Fresh or frozen raspberries or strawberries.
Raspberry or strawberry jelly.
Cream.
Cheeses.
Biscuits.
Milk and/or cream for the coffee.

Pre-Preparation

1. Make the flan, see page 232.
2. Peel the potatoes and put in cold water to cover.
3. If frozen salmon is used, make sure it is defrosted in time for the cooking.

Meal preparation

1. Set the table. Put out serving dishes and arrange to heat those needed for hot food.
2. Put out the cheese and biscuits, butter and jug of cream.
3. Forty minutes before the meal is to be served put the fish and potatoes to cook, see pages 232 and 135.
4. Make the consommé and keep it hot, see page 233.
5. Put the peas to boil: see page 132.
6. Make the hollandaise sauce and put to keep warm: see page 233.
7. Dish up fish, vegetables and sauce and put to keep warm.
8. Make the toast for the soup.
9. Add sherry or Marsala to the soup and serve.
10. Make coffee at the end of the meal.
N.B. This meal can be partly cooked with the auto-timer, the fish, potatoes and peas in casseroles.

FRESH FRUIT FLAN

QUANTITIES for 6 using 8–9 in (20–23 cm) pie plate

3 oz butter or margarine (6 Tbs or 100 g): 1 ½ Tbs golden syrup

Melt these together.

4½ oz cornflake crumbs (½ c or 130 g): 1½ oz brown sugar (3 Tbs or 45 g)

Add these to the melted mixture and combine thoroughly. Press into the pie plate to make a flan shape. Cover with foil and put in the refrigerator to chill.

1 lb ripe or defrosted raspberries or strawberries (½ kg): ½ pt raspberry or strawberry jelly (¼ l)

Allow the jelly to cool and begin to thicken. Arrange the fruit in the flan case and spoon the jelly over it. Leave to set.

Cream

Either decorate the flan with whipped cream or serve unwhipped cream in a jug.

BAKED SALMON EN PAPILOTTE

COOKING TIME: 30 mins: QUANTITIES for 6
TEMPERATURE E 375–400°, G 5–6

6 salmon steaks (6–8 oz each or 180–250 g): lemon juice: salt and pepper

Put each steak in the centre of a piece of foil. Sprinkle the fish with salt and pepper and lemon juice. Fold the foil over to make a neat parcel. Place in a baking dish and cook until tender. Remove the foil and serve any liquid with the fish.

Hollandaise sauce

Hand separately.

HOLLANDAISE SAUCE (using the blender)

¼ pt tepid water (½ c or 1½ dl): 1 oz melted butter (2 Tbs or 30 g): 3 egg yolks: 2 Tbs lemon juice: 2 sprigs parsley: ½ tsp salt: pinch of pepper

Put all the ingredients in the blender goblet and mix at full speed for 1 minute. Pour into a saucepan and heat gently until the sauce thickens, stirring all the time. Keep warm but do not allow it to continue cooking.

CHICKEN CONSOMMÉ. Make this according to the directions on the packet and just before serving add the sherry or marsala.

CHAPTER TWENTY-FIVE

Food for a Buffet Party

THESE suggestions are intended for a buffet party where the guests help themselves. For this it is necessary to have a table or tables large enough to take all the food as well as piles of plates and the forks and napkins. It is also desirable to have small tables for guests to put glasses and empty plates on and enough chairs for people to sit down if they want to. The table should be well lighted so that guests can easily see what is available and can serve themselves without having to fumble and spill food. If candles are used to light the table, they should be tall and well above and away from the food. The same applies to any floral decoration and it is often simpler to use a centre piece of fresh fruit instead of flowers.

The table can be arranged against a wall or in the centre of the room, the latter being the better method for a lot of guests.

It is better not to put all the food on the table at once but to replenish as necessary, this being particularly important for perishable foods like meat and fish, whether used alone or as sandwich or patty fillings. No food of this kind should be allowed to remain for more than half an hour in a warm room.

If hot dishes are to be served, it is necessary to have a hot-plate of some sort, heated electrically or with a spirit lamp. Hot food, too should be replenished when necessary, and no food should be kept just warm for any length of time.

Be sure there is serving cutlery beside each dish which needs it and a pile of plates and forks. Large plates are better than small ones so that guests can take small amounts of several different foods at a time.

Table napkins are better either folded and put in large tumblers or decorative jars, or placed in overlapping rows near the edge of the table, so arranged that it is easy to pick up one at a time.

Foods which can be eaten with the aid of a cocktail stick should have an egg cup or small jar containing sticks placed beside them.

BREAD-BASED SNACKS

These can be conventional sandwiches, small rounds or squares of bread with filling on top, or filled small rolls.

Sliced bread is essential for quick preparation of most of these. For variety, have some white, some brown and some of the ready-sliced rye bread sold in packets. Small plain and cheese biscuits can be used in place of bread to give variety of shape and texture.

Make sure the butter for spreading is really soft. Take it out of the refrigerator in good time or, if this has been forgotten, cut the butter in small pieces and stand it in a warm place for a while to soften but not melt.

Much time can be saved by buying ready-prepared fillings, see page 202 for suggestions.

Those which follow are for something a little different, especially for the buffet party.

QUANTITIES FOR SANDWICHES

Allow 1½–2 full rounds of sandwich per person, though this will obviously depend to some extent on the other foods being served. A small loaf usually has 16 slices and a large one 20–30 slices. A quartern loaf has 50 slices.

Four ounces of softened butter should be enough to spread one large loaf and you need 2½–3 times as much filling, but this will vary with the type of sandwich.

Suggestions for party specials

1. Fingers of rye bread spread with smoked cod's roe, obtainable canned or by the ounce from some delicatessens.
2. Small buttered biscuits topped with cheese and a round of tomato or cucumber or a piece of anchovy fillet. Use sliced cheese and stamp out rounds with a small pastry cutter.
3. Small sticks of cheese rolled in thin slices of buttered brown bread which have been spread with French mustard.
4 Asparagus tips rolled in thin brown bread and butter which has been spread with mayonnaise or salad cream.
5. Mix in the electric blender 2 oz soft butter (60 g), 2 Tbs single cream, 3 oz blue cheese (100 g), salt and pepper to taste. Use for sandwiches (unbuttered bread); or to top fingers of bread or biscuits.
6. Mix in the electric blender 4 oz soft butter (120 g), 2 Tbs single cream, 2 oz shrimp, lobster or crab (60 g). Use for sandwiches (unbuttered bread), or to top fingers of bread or biscuits.
7. Put 4 oz soft butter (120 g) in a small warm bowl and beat in 1 tsp curry powder, salt and pepper and onion or garlic juice to taste (use a garlic press). Use the mixture to spread on biscuits or to spread bread for sandwiches made with fillings of egg, shell-fish or cheese.
8. Make your own herring paste by putting roll mops in the electric blender, or use home-soused herrings, first removing the main bones.

PATTIES AND PASTRY SNACKS

You can buy ready-baked patty cases from some bakers or from the deep freeze cabinet, or make your own patty shells. For these use ready-made pastry, sold frozen or ready for use. For shaping and baking, see page 198.

SHELL FISH FILLING. Mix equal volumes of canned fresh lobster, crab, shrimps, oysters or mussels with Béchamel or tomato sauce or a concentrated soup such as tomato or mushroom.

ASPARAGUS PATTIES. Use undiluted concentrated asparagus soup with some canned asparagus tips added. Serve hot or cold.

MUSHROOM PATTIES. Use canned, undiluted concentrated mushroom soup and add some chopped and fried fresh mushrooms or some canned button mushrooms. Serve hot or cold.

CHICKEN PATTIES. Mix equal volumes of diced cooked chicken with Béchamel or tomato sauce.

Alternatively, use canned chicken in cream sauce. Serve hot. For variety, add either some canned chopped mushrooms or pimentos.

FORK AND FINGER WAYS WITH CHEESE

1. Serve cubes of cheese threaded on cocktail sticks with chunks of banana and walnut halves.
2. Serve cubes of cheese on cocktail sticks with apple wedges (dipped in lemon juice) and tiny cocktail onions.
3. Serve cubes of blue cheese on cocktail sticks with cubes of pineapple or black grapes or stuffed olives.
4. Put half an inch of chutney in a small bowl and stand short fingers of cheese upright in it.
5. Serve cubes of cheese on cocktail sticks with squares of stoned dates.
6. Sandwich walnut halves with cottage cheese.
7. Stone fat soft prunes and fill with cottage cheese mixed with mayonnaise.

COFFEE FOR 25

8 oz coarsely ground coffee (250 g): *4 pt water* (2 *l*): *8 pt milk* (4 *l*)

Put coffee and water into a saucepan and heat until it is just bubbling. Remove from the heat, stir and leave in a warm place for 5 mins. Strain into a hot jug. Heat the milk to steaming stage but do not allow a skin to form. Pour into hot jugs.

WINES FOR THE BUFFET. Some will like red and some white. For 25 people allow about five bottles of each.

Serve the red wine at room temperature and open it an hour in advance. White wines should be served chilled but not too cold.

SUGGESTIONS FOR OTHER DRINKS. See pages 208–9.

FRUIT PUNCH

QUANTITIES for 25 glasses

2 lb sugar (4 c or 1 kg): 2 qt water (8 c or 2 l)

Heat these together until the sugar dissolves.

6 oranges

Peel. Remove as much white pith as possible and cut oranges into slices. Add to the syrup.

6 more oranges: 6 lemons

Extract the juice and strain it into the syrup.

4 sliced bananas: 8 oz small green grapes, stoned (250 g): 8 oz cherries, stoned (250 g)

Add these to the rest of the mixture and chill..

1 qt ginger ale (4 c or 1 l): 1 pt cold weak tea (2 c or ½ l): 2 qt soda water (8 c or 2 l)

Just before serving, add these to the punch together with some ice cubes.

SWEETS FOR THE BUFFET

Many people do not like sweets at all but it is as well to have some available and they will help to decorate the table as well as pleasing those with a sweet tooth.

Fresh fruit salad or a compôte of fruit are usually popular. Serve in a big bowl with a small ladle for serving into fruit bowls. Have a large jug of single cream beside it.

When berries are in season, a big bowl of fresh raspberries or strawberries is indicated. Sprinkle them with caster sugar some hours before serving and stand in a cold place. Have a bowl of caster sugar and a jug of cream beside it.

Alternatively, serve defrosted frozen raspberries or strawberries.

Other simple and popular sweets are fruit flans with either a sponge or pastry base, see pages 193, 197.

CHAPTER TWENTY-SIX

Meals in the Automatic Cooker

THE automatic cooker is the greatest help to those who cannot be in the kitchen when it is time to put the meal on. It is, however, necessary to spend time earlier in the day or the night before to prepare the food and arrange it in the oven. With many things, the preparation can be done the night before and the food stored in the refrigerator until it is required.

Food which is to be put in the oven in the morning to wait until late afternoon or early evening before cooking, needs to be something which will not spoil during the storage period. It is, of course, important that the oven should be quite cold before the food is put in.

COOKING TIMES

It is usually necessary to add 10–15 minutes to the normal cooking times but if there is any chance that you will not be at hand to take the meal out when it is cooked, set the timer to switch off 15 minutes before the end of the calculated cooking time.

CHOICE OF DISHES

You probably will not want to cook more than one or two dishes for a meal in this way, but it is often convenient to cook dishes for other meals at the same time, e.g. custard or milk puddings, stewed fruit, meat casseroles (to be re-heated), and soups.

OVEN COOKED VEGETABLES

Vegetables such as potatoes which discolour after peeling should be brushed thickly and evenly with oil to exclude air. This should be done even if the vegetables are to be boiled instead of roasted. For boiling, put in a casserole, add a little cold water and see the lid fits well. Foil pressed over the top and down the sides makes a good cover.

All root vegetables, green peas, marrow and onion can be cooked this way but green vegetables such as cabbage, etc., are best cooked quickly on top of the stove just before serving the meal.

MEAT

Automatic cooking is very suitable for roasts and for most casserole dishes, for baking chops and steaks, cooking chicken most ways, including steaming with a small amount of liquid.

MILK PUDDINGS

Put these in a dish large enough to prevent boiling over and, as an extra precaution, stand the dish on a baking tray to catch any spills.

PIES AND TARTS

All are suitable for this kind of cooking. Stand the pie dish or pie plate on a baking tray to catch any juices which may bubble out.

BAKED CUSTARDS. See page 186.

BREAKFASTS IN THE AUTOMATIC OVEN

This is one of the most useful meals to cook with the auto-timer, especially if your family expect a fairly substantial hot meal. Similar foods can, of course, be cooked for supper and high tea.

Most breakfast dishes can be put in the oven the night before and timed to be cooked ready for serving.

Suitable foods include: Bacon, best rolled so that it takes longer to cook than rashers and can then be cooked with items like tomatoes and kidneys. Tomatoes halves or small whole ones. Mushrooms. Kippers wrapped in foil or in a covered dish. Quick porridge oats in a covered dish. Slices of liver. Sausages.

At the same time a dish for a later meal in the day can be cooked too, e.g. a pudding or stewed fruit, or baked apples. If it needs to be cooked longer than the breakfast dish, it can continue while breakfast is being served and cleared away.

ROLLED OATS PORRIDGE

COOKING TIME: 30–45 mins: TEMPERATURE E 350–400°, G 4–6: QUANTITIES for 4–6

6–8 oz rolled oats (1 ½–2 c or 180–250 g): 2 tsp salt

Put these in a heat-proof basin or casserole, using the larger quantity of oats for a thick porridge.

2 pt boiling water (4 c or 1 l)

Add to the oats, stir and cover with foil or a lid which fits. Put in the cold oven and set the timer. The temperature and time can be regulated to fit in with other things being cooked at the same time. Stir before serving.

KIDNEYS AND BACON with mushrooms or tomatoes.

COOKING TIME: 30–40 mins: TEMPERATURE E 375°, G 5 QUANTITIES for 4

4 sheep's kidneys: 4–8 oz mushrooms (120–250 g): 8 rashers bacon: 4–8 tomatoes

Wash and dry the kidneys and trim off fat and tubes. Remove skins. Remove bacon rinds and roll up the rashers. Wash mushrooms and remove stalks. Wash tomatoes.

Butter or oil: salt and pepper

Put all the ingredients in a pan or baking dish and put a little knob of butter in each mushroom cup, or brush with oil.

Season mushrooms and tomatoes with salt and pepper.

Put in a cold oven and set the timer. Serve with any liquid in the dish.

SAUSAGES, BACON AND TOMATOES

COOKING TIME: 30 mins: TEMPERATURE E 400°, G 6:
QUANTITIES for 4

1 *lb small pork sausages* (½ *kg*): 8 *small rashers of bacon*: 4–8 *tomatoes*

Prick the sausages and put in a baking dish. Remove rinds and roll bacon. Cut large tomatoes in half, leave small ones whole.

Put in the cold oven and set the timer.

CHAPTER TWENTY-SEVEN

Quick Light Meals

THESE include high tea, supper or lunch meals. Today even the traditional dinner meal is becoming a much lighter one for many people. This is undoubtedly partly due to the more sedentary life most of us lead and to our realisation that light meals are a way to sensible weight control and good health.

They consist of one main course with fresh, stewed or canned fruit. Additions for those who need more than this can be cheese and biscuits, bread, cake or pastry. The main dish may be complete by itself or may have vegetables or salad as accompaniments.

The important point is that this sort of meal can not only be light but quick and easy to prepare, with minimum cooking, and, therefore, a boon to the busy woman.

The fourteen suggestions which follow are for types of meals rather than specific menus. They can be used as a pattern for planning and variety can be given by using the different alternatives for the main dishes.

Most of the dishes can have a certain amount of pre-preparation and then be stored in the refrigerator until required or they can be purchased ready prepared. Suggestions for all these possibilities have been included. Soup has been suggested where the main dish is cold but can, of course, be served with any of the meals. It is assumed that this would be a packet or canned variety or one made in minutes with the electric blender.

No 1

A grill e.g. cutlets, liver, kidneys, steak, chop, fish steak, sausages, sausages, chicken, small whole fish, beef or pork burgers, see pages 81, 95, 96, 102, 104 and 111.

Grilled tomatoes and/or mushrooms
Potatoes or bread
Fruit

The ingredients for the grill can be prepared in advance and stored in the refrigerator. If frozen food is to be used, take it out of the freezer into the refrigerator in time to thaw. Many of these items can be grilled from the frozen state but results are generally better after thawing.

No 2

A pasta dish, e.g. a spaghetti or macaroni dish made quickly from raw pasta and served with ready-prepared sauce. Alternatively use a canned or packet completed dish. See pages 180–3.

A salad
Fruit

Check that you have the necessary ingredients for the pasta dish, including ready grated cheese to serve with it. The salad ingredients can be washed and stored in the refrigerator and the dressing made in advance.

No 3

A soup
Cold meat, a single one or mixed platter (see page 90)
Pickles
Salad
Bread or rolls
Fruit

If you are using canned meats, put the tin in the refrigerator to chill for easy carving. Ready cooked meat should be purchased the day of

use. Cold meat you have cooked yourself can be carved in advance
and stored in the refrigerator.

Wash the salad ingredients and store them in the refrigerator.

No 4

A vegetable dish, e.g. au gratin with a quick cheese sauce or a
ready-prepared one. Use fresh, frozen or canned vegetables. See
page 137.

Bread
Fruit

The vegetables can be prepared in advance but best results are ob-
tained if the cooking is done just before serving.

No 5

A soup
Open sandwiches, see pages 203, 236
Fruit

The completed sandwiches may be prepared in advance and stored
in the refrigerator.

No 6

A rice dish e.g. risotto, kedgeree or pilaf. Use fresh cooked, canned
or packet, see pages 174–5
Green salad
Fruit

These may all be prepared in advance and stored in the refrigerator
for re-heating or pre-prepare the ingredients. Wash the salad ingredients and store in the refrigerator.

No 7

Soup
A fish salad, see pages 142, 150–1
Fruit

The ingredients for the salad can be prepared in advance and stored in the refrigerator. If you are cooking the fish yourself, do it the day before and store in the refrigerator.

No 8

Baked fish fillets, steaks or small whole fish, cooked with a sauce over the top or serve the sauce separately. Use a quick sauce or ready prepared, see pages 53–63.

Baked jacket potatoes, see page 134
Baked tomatoes, (20 mins)
Fruit

Wash potatoes and tomatoes in advance. Make sure you have the sauce ingredients. If frozen fish is to be used, it is better to thaw it first. Fresh fish can be bought the day before and stored in the refrigerator.

No 9

A meat pie, pasty, patty or vol-au-vent
Green salad or cooked frozen vegetable
Cheese and biscuits
Fruit

This can be a ready-prepared pie to serve hot or cold or a home-made one from the freezer. Patty shells can be bought or made in advance and the filling prepared for re-heating, see page 221. If they are being served hot the salad can be a separate course, if it is preferred that way, though green salad goes well with hot pastry.

No 10

An egg dish, e.g. Omelet, mornay, curried, baked, see pages 73–7
A salad
Fruit

If a sauce is involved, it can be pre-prepared and stored in freezer or refrigerator. If ready-made is used, make sure you have enough in stock. Wash and store salad ingredients. If hard-boiled eggs are required, cook in advance and store in the refrigerator.

No 11

> *A soup*
> *A cheese board with accompaniments*, see page 66
> *Bread, rolls, biscuits*
> *Fruit*

All ingredients for this can be bought in advance and stored. It is the quickest, easiest and one of the nicest meals you can serve to cheese-lovers.

No 12

> *Fillets of fish fried in butter*, see page 81
> *Tomato and cucumber or green salad*
> *Potatoes or bread*
> *Fruit*

Prepare and wash salad in advance and store in the refrigerator. The fish may be prepared in advance and stored in the refrigerator but coat only just before cooking.

No 13

> *A soup*
> *A main dish salad*, see pages 148–52
> *Bread or rolls*
> *Fruit*

All the salad ingredients can be prepared in advance and stored in the refrigerator. Make sure the dressing is ready too, and the soup ready to heat or to be made quickly with the blender.

No 14

> *Baked chicken*, see pages 109 or 117
> *Potatoes or bread*
> *Boiled frozen vegetable*
> *Fruit*

The chicken can be prepared in advance and stored in the refrigerator.

Index